ARCO

D1118216

7 MINUTE RESUMES

DANA MORGAN

IDG Books Worldwide, Inc.
An International Data Group Company
Foster City, CA • Chicago, IL • Indianapolis, IN • New York, NY

First Edition

IDG Books Worldwide, Inc.
An International Data Group Company
919 E. Hillsdale Boulevard
Suite 400
Foster City, CA 94404

An Arco Book

For general information on IDG Books Worldwide's books in the U.S., please
call our Consumer Customer Service department at 800-762-2974. For reseller
information, including discounts and premium sales, please call our Reseller
Customer Service department at 800-434-3422.

Library of Congress information available on request

ISBN: 0-02-863701-1

Manufactured in the United States of America

10 9 8 7 6 5 4 3 2 1

TABLE OF CONTENTS

ACKNOWLEDGMENTS

To Joel—for remaining calm and steady in the midst of wide-spread upheaval.

To Kiera, Taylor, Chase, and Garrick—for their patience and fun-loving spirits.

To my parents—without whose constant assistance I couldn't have written this book.

To Grandma and Grandpa Morgan—who selfless-ly provided help and support.

To Lisa Ruffalo, Debbie Ostrowski, Sally Campbell, and all the professionals at Manchester Partners International—who join me in the mission to find great jobs for great people.

To all the hard-working job seekers that I have had the pleasure to work with—may you all achieve great success in your exciting career adventures!

CHAPTER 1

Getting Started

In this chapter, you will learn about the top new trends in resume usage and how to prepare to write an outstanding resume.

WHAT IS A RESUME?

A resume is a document that gathers your most outstanding career highlights and presents them in an easy-to-read format for potential employers to peruse. A good resume is not a mere chronicle of your work history. It offers you a chance to showcase your skills and quantify your achievements so that you introduce yourself to an employer at your best.

Think of a resume as a marketing brochure, an advertising piece, or a 30-second commercial that is selling a product. The target audience for your marketing campaign is the hiring managers and human resources coordinators who have jobs to fill. The product, of course, is you.

As with any advertisement, your marketing strategy must capture the attention of your audience. In that initial quick scan, they must be captivated by your presentation so that they want to devote the time to read on. Thus, it must be appealing to the eye, informative for the mind, and engaging in a way that grabs the reader's curiosity.

No one has ever told me that a resume is an easy thing to write. It takes a great amount of research, introspection, and planning and probably five or six rough drafts before the final version takes shape.

Yet the great pains you must go through are not wasted. If you are soon to be entering the job market, writing a resume is a valuable exercise for many reasons:

- Preparing a resume serves as a useful exercise in reviewing your background and discerning what it is you want to do and where you want to do it.

- Writing a resume can help you discover unrecognized or overlooked personal strengths. Seeing them in written form helps to solidify them.

- Answering newspaper ads and responding to job leads is a lot easier with a standard resume written, proofed, and ready to send. Think how time-consuming it would be if you had to rewrite your entire job history every time you wrote a letter to a job lead!

- The resume serves as a "cheat sheet" to help you remember dates, experiences, and other aspects of your work history in the interview. It is useful information to review before the interview and to use as a reference while the interview is taking place.

- A resume puts you and the hiring manager on the same page. You know exactly what he or she knows about you at the start of the interview. You can add the pertinent details that relate to a particular position in your face-to-face discussion.

HOW HIRING MANAGERS USE RESUMES

Hiring managers require resumes to give them specific information on potential job candidates. Resumes allow managers to compare personal qualities and job skills from one resume to another and to rate candidates according to how well they match the job specifications. Those candidates with the strongest match are chosen for an interview.

The typical employer receives an average of 400 resumes in response to an advertised job opening. Rather than conducting an interview with each respondent, he or she will use the resume as a screening tool to determine which candidates make the cut. Usually, only the top five or six candidates make it to the interview stage. These daunting statistics illustrate the need to have an outstanding resume that sets you apart from the crowd.

TOP NEW TRENDS IN RESUMES

Resumes have changed in style and complexity over the years, just as clothing styles change and yield to trends in the fashion industry. In the same way that last year's skirt length might now be out of date, the resume you used to land your last position might no longer be the right "fit" for today's employers.

Hiring managers now concentrate their attention on different personal qualities and skill sets as compared with resumes in the past. In response to this change, resumes have taken on a new form.

What Today's Employers Look for in a Resume

- **Today's employers look for specifics.** They want to know what your specific skills are and how you applied those skills in your most recent positions. They don't want all the details of your past jobs; they want the hard, practical skills filtered out and labeled for them.

- **Today's employers want the resume in simple, small bites.** They want to be able to scan the page and glean the important information quickly and easily. They no longer want to spend time wading through long paragraphs filled with tedious details.

- **Today's employers want proof of performance.** They want to see numbers and results in your resume to show that you can save the company time or money.

- **Today's employers expect examples to substantiate your claims.** They want to see that you have had successes and can achieve results.

- **Today's employers want a good communicator.** They will scrutinize your resume for spelling or grammatical errors and study it for phrasing. They want to know that you write well, because more and more jobs involve writing skills. They will also look for evidence of oral communications skills, because this is a growing trend in the work world as well.

- **Today's employers want a strong team player.** This is not so much a variation from the past, as it is a continuation of it. More than ever, employers realize that an employee who cannot work well with others is more of a hindrance than a help. They will scan your resume for evidence of a positive relationship with coworkers.

Other Hot Spots on Today's Resumes

- **A strong summary** More and more employers expect to find the highlights of the resume placed in a central spot where they can be found at a glance. If employers feel they have to wade through the entire resume to decipher the important stuff, they might not bother (see chapter 7).

- **Current training** The trend in today's workplace is toward keeping your job-related skills fresh. Technical skills, especially, must not appear outdated. Employers will scan resumes for recent training, courses, or workshops that keep your skills up to date.

- **Community involvement** Employers like to know that you are a well-rounded person and an active member of your community. They might look for evidence of community involvement at the bottom of your resume.

- **The cover letter** Employers know that many job seekers have a resume professionally written for them these days, which gives the resume reader fewer clues regarding the applicant's writing ability and style. Therefore, the employers are likely to turn to the cover letter for these clues, so write it carefully! (See chapter 20.)

 The cover letter will be scrutinized for spelling, grammar, and phrasing. Take the time to write it well!

Five Common Misconceptions about Resumes

1. **A good resume can land you a good job.** Resumes do not land you a job. They land you an interview perhaps, but landing the job is up to you. I know of no case where a job seeker was offered a job based on his or her resume alone.

 Your resume is simply your introduction into the world of job possibilities. It is only one small piece of the job search process.

2. **A resume must include information about all previous jobs.** Happily, a resume need not include complete information about all jobs ever held, or employers would be forced to wade through several minimum wage starter jobs to get to the positions that they feel are pertinent. A thorough resume includes information about all jobs going back 10 to 15 years, unless a job lasted for a brief time. Beyond 10 to 15 years, jobs can be given a slight mention, grouped together under one title, or eliminated altogether.

3. **Resumes must be tweaked in response to particular positions.** Not so. Don't waste your time rewriting your resume to fit the details of various jobs. The rule is: Write ONE good resume that highlights the most successful aspects of your experience and skills. Save the "tweaking" for the cover letter, which you have to rewrite in response to individual ads anyway.

   Of course, if you discover a job opening that appeals to you and you worry that your resume is ill fitted to the position, go ahead and restructure it to highlight skills and accomplishments that are more appropriate. This should be the exceptional case, however, rather than the rule.

4. **To look its best, a resume should be done by a professional.** With today's high-powered PCs and excellent word-processing programs, it is no longer difficult to create an impressive looking document at home.

5. **A resume must be restricted to one page.** Today's resumes can be up to two pages in length, if two pages are necessary to convey the highlights of your past positions. More than two pages, however, is a no-no.

BEFORE YOU START WRITING

Before putting pen to paper, it is a good idea to research your background and collect the data you need. Make sure you do the legwork to have concrete data on hand as you write.

 The single greatest weakness in most resumes is vagueness!

Some things you might need to gather are:

- Job descriptions from past or present positions
- Performance reviews
- Reports and presentations that you have written
- Documents, brochures, and reports that you have designed
- School records and transcripts
- Military certificates of service
- Newspaper or newsletter clippings about you
- Letters of recommendation
- Letters of appreciation from clients, customers, colleagues, or superiors

It is best to gather all of the information you will be using for all sections of the resume before you begin writing any piece of it. This way, you have your information organized and ready to go when the time comes to plug it in place.

Gather all records and paperwork before you begin writing so your work progresses smoothly with fewer interruptions.

Checklist of Resume Information

Prepare a checklist by dividing the resume into sections and listing the information that you will need to include in each part. Cross things off after you've done your research on each topic.

The checklist of information below should help you get started. Be sure to add items to the list or delete others to fit your situation.

Resume Heading

The resume heading simply gives the potential employer the ability to contact you as easily as possible.

Information you will need:

- ☐ Your name
- ☐ Address
- ☐ Telephone number
- ☐ Cell phone/beeper/voice mail (optional)
- ☐ Fax number (optional)
- ☐ E-mail address (optional)

Summary

The summary offers the reader a quick overview of your background and skills; it is a brief profile of your strengths.

Information you will need:

- ☐ Your list of intuitive skills (from chapter 2)
- ☐ Your list of learned skills (from chapter 2)
- ☐ Knowledge of your career goals (from chapter 3)

Experience

The Experience section gives the potential employer a look at your work history in chronological order.

Information you will need:

- ☐ Inclusive dates of employment
- ☐ Names of companies for which you worked
- ☐ City and state in which company was located
- ☐ Your job title(s)
- ☐ Long-term projects or assignments you were involved in

Education

The Education section lists the educational institutions you attended and the degrees you earned.

Information you will need:

- ☐ Name of college(s) or university(ies) attended
- ☐ City and state of institution(s)
- ☐ Dates of attendance
- ☐ Degrees earned
- ☐ Honors or awards achieved
- ☐ Grade-point-average (if above 3.4)

Courses and Training

The Courses and Training section lists the educational opportunities you have had outside of your formal schooling.

Information you will need:

- ☐ Courses, workshops, or seminars attended
- ☐ Company-sponsored training classes
- ☐ Technical classes

Other

You might need to include other sections on your resume to capture the full scope of your skills and knowledge.

Information you will need:

- ☐ Professional organizations and associations
- ☐ Community organizations in which you are involved
- ☐ Foreign languages you speak fluently
- ☐ Outstanding achievements outside of work
- ☐ Licenses or accreditations earned
- ☐ Publications or patents

Military Service

This section offers a brief record of your military service. This information is optional.

Information you will need:

- ☐ Branch of military
- ☐ Dates of service
- ☐ Highest rank achieved

CHAPTER SUMMARY

In this chapter, you learned the basics of today's resumes and began a checklist to gather the information you need to begin writing your resume.

CHAPTER 2

Know Your Accomplishments and Skills

In this chapter, you complete a personal assessment worksheet to help you identify your likes and dislikes. This enables you to write a resume that is reflective of your strengths and achievements.

Many people assume that the first step to writing a resume is to buy the paper, sharpen the pencils, and go at it from there. However, to write a resume that truly reflects who you are and what your unique qualities are, you must do a bit of inward reflection first.

The following exercise will help you take your personal history that you have been storing in the back part of your brain and bring it to the forefront for review. You will most likely be amazed at how little you remembered about your past achievements until you dusted them off by working through this exercise!

This is an important first step in writing your resume. You will use the accomplishments and skills that you identify to enhance the main body of your resume.

YOUR ACCOMPLISHMENTS

An accomplishment is something that:

- You did well
- You enjoyed doing
- Involved a problem that you solved
- You are proud of

Accomplishments begin with situations or problems that call for action. You have taken steps to alleviate the problems, thereby achieving results.

An accomplishment does not have to relate to your school or work experience. It can be anything from your personal background as well. Some examples are:

- Planned a trip and traveled to Europe solo
- Coordinated a conference for 180 people
- Directed the annual PTA fund-raiser

These are specific projects you took on at work, school, home, or in the community.

 Don't overlook the results portion of your accomplishments. Employers will key in on results.

YOUR SKILLS

You can't write a good poem without having good writing skills. You can't direct a successful program without having good leadership skills. Each of your accomplishments can be broken down into a set of skills that you used in realizing the accomplishment.

Don't be shy! Employers want to know if you have the skills to accomplish a particular job for them. If you integrate some of your key accomplishments into the interview, employers will discern the skills that you have and assess whether you can put those same skills to use for them.

The Two Types of Skills

Employers attempt to assess two types of skills during an interview.

Learned Skills

Learned skills are those skills that you have been taught or that you have taught yourself somewhere along the way. They might be related to your current career, past positions, or other aspects of your life.

Examples of learned skills are:

Rebuilding a car engine

Driving a bus

Planting a garden

Running a computer program

Hanging drywall

Sewing a dress

Managing a product line

All of these skills involve learning new behaviors and gaining knowledge about the way things work and the steps involved in making certain things happen. In none of these cases could a person know how to do these things without first learning how.

Learned skills are not necessarily technological or career-related. Cooking a gourmet dinner is just as much a skill as launching a satellite; both involve learned processes and behaviors. A potential employer, however, is most interested in the learned skills that are closely related to the position for which you are applying.

Intuitive Skills

Intuitive skills are those skills that you possess innately; they are a part of your personality, and you are able to use these skills in many different situations.

Examples of intuitive skills are:

Persistence

Tidiness

Efficiency

Creativity

Tenacity

Honesty

Precision

Adaptability

Punctuality

These are personality traits that you carry with you throughout life. As you can see, they are less specific than the learned skills, but they are no less important. These skills are transferable from one situation to the next—if you are honest in one situation, you are likely to be honest in another. Punctual people can be counted on to arrive on time, no matter what the setting or situation.

Know your intuitive skills! Potential employers often pay more attention in the interview to intuitive skills than they do to learned skills. You must be ready with a defined skills list if you are to do well in the interview.

ASSESSMENT

Identifying your own skills and strengths is not difficult. Follow the four steps of this simple exercise and compile your personal skills list.

1. List Your Six Favorite Accomplishments

These can be from any time in your life and can be as detailed or as simple as you want. You might include accomplishments from a childhood scouting project, the time you stood up to the bully on the playground, or the million-dollar account you landed last July.

Example:

> When I was 22 and had just graduated from college, I talked a group of my friends into spending six months with me on a backpacking trip of Europe. We had no money, no contacts, and very little knowledge, but we went anyway and had a ball.

2. Examine Why This Accomplishment Makes You Satisfied or Proud

Write your thoughts below each accomplishment.

Example:

> I was able to convince my friends to spend a great amount of effort and time on a project I had conceived.
>
> I had to do extensive research, planning, and coordinating just to get things off the ground.
>
> It was a courageous thing to do.
>
> I managed to get along in many different countries that had customs and languages different from those of the U.S.

We survived for six months on practically no money. I came up with a few ingenious ways to save cash.

The five of us got along great for the entire six months despite close quarters, differing agendas, and dissimilar personalities.

It was a long-term project that I stuck with, despite a lack of support and other problems.

I learned to deal with foreign currency and various rates of exchange.

3. Filter Out the Skills

Examine each statement to discern the skills involved. Include even those skills that seem obvious or simple. List the skills on a separate sheet of paper.

 Don't overlook your basic skills. Many people who are assessing their skills overlook the most basic ones because they figure everyone has them and they are not worth listing. Remember that not everyone can do what you can do. Take care to include all skills.

Example:

1. **Convinced my friends** Persuasion, tenacity, salesmanship, enthusiasm, and ability to motivate others

2. **Planned details of the trip** Ability to conduct research, plan, coordinate, and arrange; organizational skills

3. **Did it even though I was a little bit afraid** Courage, risk-taking, boldness, and self-confidence

4. **Adjusted to new customs** Adaptability, flexibility, and ability to learn

5. **Survived six months on a tiny budget** Ability to manage a budget, economical, and conservative

6. **Maintained friendships**   Ability to compromise, respectful of friendships, outgoing, and get along well with others

7. **Stuck with long-term project**   Determination, focus, drive, tenacity, vision, persistence, and self-confidence

8. **Learned foreign currency**   Attention to detail and knowledge of exchange rates

The backpacking trip accomplishment easily involves well over 30 skills that are vital to success in any professional position. Interviewers will be looking for these types of skills. In completing this exercise, you are preparing yourself with a list of your skills ready for the asking. Moreover, you have in hand more than a list of words—you have organized the proof (the accomplishments themselves) to back up the words!

4. Identify Your Most Predominant Skills

As you complete this exercise, some skills reappear under almost every accomplishment. These skills are a strong part of your personal skill set. Write the 10 most frequently occurring technical skills and the 10 most frequent intuitive skills below:

10 Technical Skills

_____

_____

_____

_____

_____

_____

_____

_____

_____

_____

10 Intuitive Skills

_____

_____

_____

_____

_____

_____

_____

_____

_____

CHAPTER SUMMARY

In this chapter, you learned to identify your unique accomplishments and skills using the four-step skills assessment exercise. You also learned why all your skills and accomplishments are important to include on your resume.

CHAPTER 3

Setting Career Goals

In this chapter, you identify the direction that your career path should be heading. It will enable you to write a clearer, more focused resume by helping you to narrow your job objective.

SETTING YOUR JOB OBJECTIVE

An employment manager can spot an unfocused job seeker a mile away. In an interview, it is obvious through ambiguous answers to such questions as, "What are your job goals?" or "Where do you see yourself in five years?"

However, the resume can reveal a wishy-washy job seeker just as clearly as a poorly answered interview question. If you enter into the resume-writing phase without first focusing in on the direction you want your career to take, your final product will surely reflect your muddled career goals. To produce a resume that will impress any hiring manager with your organization and strong career goals, you must first take the time to identify your career objective.

Do not attempt to write your resume without first developing a clear vision of what you want to do. If YOU don't know, an employer certainly won't know either.

Keeping in mind the identified accomplishments and the results of your skills assessment in chapter 2, write brief answers to the following questions:

What past job experience would you like to draw upon in your next career?

_____

_____

_____

What job functions have you held in the past that you would like to avoid in future jobs?

_____

_____

_____

Which job-related activities do you do best?

_____

_____

_____

Which of your top ten intuitive skills would you like to use most?

_____

_____

_____

Which of your top ten technical skills would you like to draw upon most?

_____

_____

_____

What level of responsibility would you like to have in your next position? (Entry-level, mid-level, supervisory, and so on)

_____

_____

_____

What is your geographical preference for your next position?

_____

_____

_____

Would you like to travel? How much?

_____

_____

_____

What type of industry interests you? (Service, manufacturing, finance, sales, and so forth)

_____

_____

_____

Would you prefer to work for a small, mid-size, or large company?

_____

_____

_____

What kind of corporate culture do you prefer, formal or informal?

_____

_____

_____

Disregarding salary, what would be your ultimate fantasy fun job?

_____

_____

_____

What are your strongest interests and hobbies outside of the world of work?

_____

_____

_____

In what career areas would you most like to grow?

_____

_____

_____

A Values Exercise

Rank the following job factors according to their importance to you (1 = Most Important, 10 = Least Important).

_____ An outstanding salary

_____ A flexible work schedule to allow time for outside interests

_____ A job that allows you independence

_____ The chance to be creative at work

_____ Prestige or status in your career

_____ A job that ensures growth and challenge

_____ A position in which you work with other people

_____ A job offering a sense of responsibility and control

_____ Variety in your job

_____ A job that is low-stress

What else is of high importance to you in your next position?

_____

_____

_____

 These values should not be written directly into your resume. You will use them to help give your resume the tone and direction that reflect your strongest values.

WRITING YOUR JOB GOALS STATEMENT

After having considered the questions above, formalize your answers by writing a personal job goals statement in the space below. Describe the job that you want to do next, could do well, and would enjoy doing. It should be as detailed and as specific as possible, and it should draw upon the skills, accomplishments, and values identified in the preceding exercises.

Example 1:

I would like a supervisory-level procurement position that will incorporate my background in the manufacturing/machine tools industry. I would like to be in charge of at least 10 part-time or full-time staff and to have full responsibility for the scheduling and day-to-day oversight of the staff. This would draw upon my organization and planning skills and my strengths in working with people and motivating them to work efficiently for the company. I would also like to continue direct negotiations with vendors, to keep my skills in this area sharp.

The ideal position would be with a large manufacturing organization with international ties to incorporate my expertise in foreign markets and to allow travel opportunities. I would thrive in an informal corporate culture and a management structure that enables me to make decisions and work independently.

I would prefer the possibility of upward growth and salary advancement within the organization so that I can enjoy a feeling of stability and plant my feet firmly in the new company. I am looking for variety, responsibility, a sense of teamwork, and a chance to be creative.

 As you write your personal goals statement, remember that this is for your eyes only. It will not go on your resume, and no one else need ever see it. It is simply for your own clarification!

Example 2:

I would like an entry-level administrative position with a small medical or dental office in my local area. I hope to have direct contact with patients at the desk, and I would enjoy some receptionist duties along with secretarial and record-keeping responsibilities. These things would draw on my strong organizational skills but also allow me some variety and a chance to work with people.

I would like a stable, quiet environment without the high-pressure atmosphere of my last job. I especially want a flexible work schedule, to give me freedom to attend the kids' basketball games.

I hope for an office that has advanced computer systems so that I can learn more about working with word processing and spreadsheet applications. I would like an informal work environment and a relaxed atmosphere among coworkers. I would be happy with a salary slightly above my last position, but I am in need of an excellent benefits package.

WORKSHOP

Use this template to help you formulate your personal job goals statement:

For my next position, I would like a _____ (level)
job in the _____ industry. I would like to manage
_____ (number) of staff, and be responsible for
_____ (duties). This would draw upon these skills of
mine: _____, _____, and _____.

The ideal position would be with a _____ (size)
organization. I would thrive in a _____ corporate
culture. I like a management structure that enables me
to _____.

I'm looking for these things from my job:

_____

_____

_____

CHAPTER SUMMARY

In this chapter, you mapped out a job objective using your identified accomplishments and skills from chapter 2. You also examined your values and used them to help you write a realistic and focused personal job goals statement.

CHAPTER 4

Resume Styles

In this chapter, you learn key visual strategies to give your resume an easy-to-read professional appearance that will please the eye of any hiring manager. You also learn the most common mistakes in resume format and how to avoid them.

STANDARD RESUME STYLES

Hiring managers value a standardized format because it makes the resume quicker to scan if the information is laid out in a predictable fashion. If every resume put the Education section in a different place, for example, it would be much more time-consuming to search for this information.

Over the years, a couple of resume formats have emerged that tend to appeal to hiring managers for their simple and logical design.

Successful resumes—those that land interviews—come in only two formats:

1. The chronological resume

2. The functional resume

The Chronological Resume

The chronological resume lists your employment by date with your most recent job shown first, followed by a brief description of the job(s) you held there. A well-written chronological resume also emphasizes accomplishments at each job. See the example below.

JILL PETERS

531 Fall Terrace   Parkton, TN 09734   (709) 555-3421

SUMMARY

Dedicated sales management professional with over 16 years experience in research, promotion, and management. Known for friendly attitude, organized approach, and perseverance in all aspect of sales campaign. Special skills in:

- Staff Management
- Promotional Campaigns
- Market Research
- Media Advertising
- Training and Development
- Manufacturing sales

EXPERIENCE

Sales Promotion Manager, Ross Tristate, Inc. Kings, TN 1994-1999

Developed and supervised sales promotion projects for large businesses and manufacturers in the plastics industry. Hired and supervised 22 sales staff on a local and regional basis.

- Wrote and coordinated media advertising and organized sales promotion strategies with public relations.

- Assisted in the establishment of 6 branch offices throughout the southern U.S., including hiring personnel and staff development.

- Designed, wrote, and presented sales training program to district and regional sales staff, which received excellent feedback from attendees and management.

Sales Administrator, Solon Kline Company, Wexam, TN 1989-1994

Conducted market research and studied efficiency of sales program to coordinate regional offices and establish efficient communication and effective sales campaigns.

- Devised and supervised market research projects to determine sales potential and advertising needs.

- Wrote recommendations for improved distribution, areas of developments, and sales potential.

- Improved catalog system for inventory control which facilitated stock movement and resulted in $3M savings to company.

EDUCATION

Tennessee State University, Gatlin, TN   BA, Chemistry 1983

The Functional Resume

The functional resume emphasizes your accomplishments and is divided into categories by job function rather than by date. It de-emphasizes the names of the companies for which you have worked, the dates of employment, and the amount of time you have spent in each job.

See the example below.

JILL PETERS

531 Fall Terrace   Parkton, TN 09734   (709) 555-3421

SUMMARY
Dedicated sales management professional with over 16 years experience in research, promotion, and management. Known for friendly attitude, organized approach, and perseverance in all aspects of sales campaign. Special skills in:

- Staff management
- Promotional campaigns
- Market Research

* Media advertising
* Training and Development
* Manufacturing sales

SALES EXPERIENCE

- Hired and supervised 22 sales staff on local and regional basis.

- Assisted in the establishment of 6 branch offices throughout the southern U.S., including hiring personnel and staff development

MANAGEMENT

- Designed, wrote, and presented sales training program to district and regional sales staff, which received excellent feedback from attendees and management.

- Improved catalog system for inventory control which facilitated stock movement and resulted in $3M savings to company.

- Devised and supervised market research projects to determine sales potential and advertising needs.

RESEARCH

- Wrote recommendations for improved distribution, areas of development, and sales potential.

- Supervised sales promotion projects for large business firms and manufacturers in the plastics industry.

PROMOTION

- Wrote and coordinated media advertising and organized sales promotion strategies with public relations.

EMPLOYMENT HISTORY

1994-1999   **Sales Promotion Manager**, Ross Tristate, Inc. Kings, TN

1989-1994   **Sales Administrator,** Solon Kline Company, Wexam, TN

1983-1989   **Salesman,** Foxdale Industrial Plastics, Foxdale, GA

EDUCATION   **Tennessee State University,** Gatlin, TN
                              BA, Chemistry   1983

Functional resumes have developed a bad reputation over the years. They have been used to hide negatives such as multiple firings, extended unemployment, and chronically poor job records. Some employment managers, therefore, have become suspicious of resumes written in the functional format. To alleviate these fears, be sure to include a full employment section on the functional resume, which includes names of companies you have worked for and dates of employment.

CHOOSING THE RIGHT RESUME STYLE FOR YOU

The chronological resume is by far the most common resume format used today. It enables the reader to identify information quickly, and to review your employment history in an orderly time sequence. As trends come and go, the accomplishments-based chronological resume has emerged as the most successful resume type. The prevailing school of thought, therefore, leans strongly toward using the chronological resume, unless there is a compelling reason not to use it.

Chronological Resumes Should Be Used If:

- You have spent three or more successful years with previous employers and have not changed jobs frequently.
- You have a stable career background, and you are seeking a position in the same field or a related field.
- You have worked for companies that have positive name recognition.
- Your resume can demonstrate steady growth in job responsibilities and career level.

Functional Resumes Should Be Used If:

- You have a non-linear career track that does not show upward growth.
- You are seeking a job in a field that is radically different from your current career.
- You are re-entering the job market after an absence of several years.
- You have limited work experience.
- You want to emphasize a job experience that was not your most recent position.

CREATING A VISUAL KNOCKOUT

After you have chosen a style of resume, it is time to consider the resume format. Choose a format that is visually pleasing, yet practical for your needs. Consider these examples:

Example 1

Notice the pleasing balance of Example 1. Your eye is drawn to the information on the left margin, which nicely separates the resume categories. This does not provide as much space on the page, however, as Example 2.

Example 2

Example 2 makes better use of the full page, and can be a better choice if the writer has an extensive career history.

Example 3

The third example has the introductions centered with the information blocked at the left margin.

Example 4

Example 4 is a functional resume format, with space in the upper portion for functional skills and longer paragraphs at the bottom to describe specific positions.

Choosing the Layout

A resume can be the most well-written piece of work ever compiled, yet if it lacks an appealing presentation, it will fail to make it past the initial screening. As you design the layout of your resume, consider these eye-catching suggestions.

Eight Key Visual Techniques:

1. **Do not stray from the standard $8^{1}/2'' \times 11''$ paper.** This is not the way to be noticed; it is the way to be ignored.

2. **Use a quality bond 20# paper in white or off white.** This gives the most traditional look to your resume. A dark color paper can be hard to read. On the other hand, a bold or fluorescent hue can be a real turnoff and looks unprofessional.

    As you choose paper color, keep in mind that many companies run resumes through optical scanners (see chapter 17), which have a difficult time reading print on darker paper. The lighter color keeps your resume scanner-friendly.

3. **Don't write more than two pages.** The ideal resume is as crisp and concise as possible without sacrificing important information. A good rule to remember is "the most persuasive message in the smallest space." If the resume can be written well in one page, all the better. A two-page resume is still acceptable, but more than two pages is considered verbose.

 Employers tend to be turned off by long-winded resumes that ramble beyond two pages.

4. **Do not shrink the typeface to fit more words on the page.** I've seen resumes that were kept to two pages simply because the type-face had been shrunk to unreadable proportions. Making the typeface microscopic isn't fooling anyone into thinking that you did a good editing job. Keep the type no less than 10 pt.

5. **Keep the margins no less than an inch at the sides, top, and bottom.** This white space frames your resume nicely and prevents the page from looking overcrowded.

6. **Use a quality printer to print your resumes.** Using a low-quality printer will get your resume noticed but not the way you want it to be noticed!

7. **Don't overuse attention-getters like boldface, underlining, and italics.** The resume should be set up to present a crisp, professional image. Too many asterisks or exclamation points can make you look over zealous and immature.

8. **Use bullets to draw the reader's eye.** Bullets are indented dots or dashes that attract the attention of the reader to the places you want him or her to see.

The Five Most Common Mistakes in Resume Format:

1. **Using too many pages** No, you are not the exception to the rule. Two pages maximum. Period.

2. **Telling the whole story in paragraph form** A page full of words squeezed in from margin to margin with no white space is not an inviting prospect to read.

 Remember, you must create the visual impression of quick bites of information that are easy to read.

3. **Telling the whole story in bullets** Because using bullets to highlight important information has become the trend, many people take this too far and write the entire page in bullet form. This negates the whole purpose of the bullets, because they no longer highlight anything.

4. **Cramming too much information into too little space** Some resume writers work so desperately to include every detail about their work history that they write a virtually unreadable resume. You must edit ruthlessly!

5. **Creating an unbalanced presentation** The inconsistent placement of resume categories can create a confusing and awkward record of your background. Keep all the tab placements for categories and headings consistent.

CHAPTER SUMMARY

In this chapter, you learned the resume styles that work best and several visual tricks to make the most of your resume presentation.

CHAPTER 5

Know What the Employer Wants to See

In this chapter, you discover how employers screen resumes and what they look for when evaluating job candidates. You then learn how to focus your resume on the intuitive and technical skills that employers value.

EVALUATING JOB CANDIDATES BY RESUME

No two hiring managers are exactly alike. This makes it tough to know what will make a resume reader jump for joy and what might turn him or her off. One person's ideal job candidate is another person's instant rejection.

There are certain factors, however, that are commonly regarded as positive qualities, no matter what the job is or who is reading the resume. It is important to know what these qualities are and how to write them into your resume.

Hiring managers typically evaluate a job candidate along two broad dimensions: job expertise and personal skills. Job expertise is a job candidate's level of knowledge, skills, industry-related experience, and technical expertise as it relates to the job at hand. Personal skills, on the other hand, are a candidate's unique set of personal behaviors and values, which allow him or her to achieve success in the particular position to be filled.

Most people assume that hiring managers place the strongest emphasis on a job candidate's level of experience (job expertise) when evaluating resumes. In reality, though, it is the personal qualities that go *beyond* the experience level that separate the mediocre job candidates from the hot prospects.

Focus on your achievements. Don't neglect to state your accomplishments and outstanding work performance boldly on the resume. These are the things that will separate you from the crowd of other resumes.

Although technical skills, job-related knowledge, and prior job experience are certainly a vital part of any resume, an experienced hiring manager uses these factors only in the first round of cuts.

What separates the technically qualified applicants from each other are the personal skills that the resume conveys, which are consistent with successful job performance. After all, it is generally easy to teach a motivated person to become successful in many job functions regardless of prior training, but it is difficult to teach an unmotivated person to be dedicated and hardworking in any job function.

Hiring managers believe that they can teach technical skills much more easily than they can teach new behaviors.

QUALITIES THAT HIRING MANAGERS LOOK FOR
Job-Related Skills

The first round of resume screening is strongly based on the level of job knowledge that each candidate possesses and the learned skills that relate to the position requirements.

How to Write It

Be sure to make reference to all skills you used in your past positions regardless of how unimportant they seem. The fact that you gave presentations to large groups might not seem to relate to a systems analyst position, for example, yet that proof of strong communications skills might be the key factor that makes you stand out from the others.

 When in doubt whether to include a skill on your resume, include it!

A Strong Work Ethic

A resume of 10 or 15 years ago might have been considered well written and thoroughly done if it included a detailed list of your daily job duties within each position you held. Today's resumes aren't considered complete without a thorough description of the accomplishments you achieved *beyond* your everyday duties. This shows the resume reader that you not only know how to do your job, but you know how to do it *well.*

How to Write It

Under each job experience that you list, include only a brief description of your daily tasks and duties. Spend the better part of the space describing what you personally contributed to the position by highlighting your accomplishments, special assignments you worked on, projects you managed or assisted with, or outstanding awards you received (see chapter 9 for details).

Enthusiasm

A hiring manager wants to hire an employee who has enthusiasm and energy for the job.

How to Write It

Use peppy language that conveys a positive attitude. For example, instead of:

"Answer phones, take calls from customers on 10-line phone system."

write it this way:

> "Enjoy dealing deftly and courteously with customers on busy
> 10-line phone system."

 Keep your resume from being dry and lifeless by infusing it with a fresh tone. Give the idea that you love your job!

Written Communication Skills

A hiring manager will assess your resume according to your written presentation. Do you have the ability to state things in a logical fashion? Are you able to use words to their best advantage? How is your spelling? Is your resume grammatically correct?

How to Write It

Don't rely solely on your computer's spell-check program to catch spelling mistakes. This can leave you with embarrassing errors that the spell-check program left behind. Have two or three friends proofread it, and ask them for feedback regarding clarity and wordiness.

 State everything as simply as possible when writing your resume.

People Skills

Although it is true that the phrase "people skills" has been overused and borders on trite, it is still a quality that hiring managers value highly. An employee without the ability to get along with coworkers or clients often causes more headaches than he or she is worth.

 Conveying a friendly attitude scores big points with any resume reader who has a job to fill.

How to Write It

Highlight accomplishments or job duties that center on dealing with people. Making oral presentations, leading meetings, negotiating contracts, acting as liaison, and supervising staff all require an ability to interact with people. Remember to emphasize not only that you did these things but also that you did them well.

Honesty

No employer wants to hire someone who is conniving, irresponsible, or deceitful. A resume must make the reader feel that the candidate has integrity.

How to Write It

Although it is always a nice touch to quantify accomplishments with percentages and statistics, it is not wise to embellish achievements by making up numbers or overstating your results. This is often quite transparent to a seasoned resume reviewer. Rather than coming across as a high achiever, you make it clear that you are willing to toy with the truth.

 If you are unsure of exact figures or percentages when quantifying results, it is safe to use the word "approximately" to indicate that the numbers might not be precise.

Confidence

As a resume writer, you must walk a fine line between conveying pride in accomplishments and appearing to have an overinflated ego. You must reach the right balance of stating your achievements without appearing to be bragging.

How to Write It

Avoid words that make high claims unless you back them up with proof. For example, don't say, "*superior*" management skills without then detailing job experience and specific results that support your claim.

Organizational Skills

Resume readers can't help but notice your organizational presentation as they read what you've written. They will evaluate your organizational capabilities and be impressed with a resume that conveys orderliness and linear thinking.

How to Write It

Make sure your resume follows a consistent format. Set up each job experience in the exact same way as the one preceding it. Set all headings and margins consistently, to create harmonious lines and a pleasing appearance.

A Positive Personality

It is difficult to assess a person's personality from a resume alone. Resumes are not designed to delve into personality traits, and after all your work experience, education, and so forth have been presented, there usually isn't much space left over to devote to personal characteristics. Remember, however, that the more you can reveal about *who you are* as opposed to *what you can do,* the more comfortable they will feel with how well you can work for *them.*

How to Write It

Feel free to give the reader as many clues as you can about your positive personality traits. Use descriptive words like "creative" or "motivated," and then be sure to include accomplishments that prove you are what you say you are!

 Refer to chapters 2 and 3 to help you choose accurate descriptive words.

Up-to-Date

Employers like to know that you are keeping current in your field and that you care enough about your skills to keep them from growing stale.

How to Write It

Include all company-sponsored training, workshops, classes, and seminars that relate to your field. Be sure to also include training in general business skills.

 Your participation in training and classes indicates to the resume reader that you have not become lazy or bored and that you are diligent about improving or increasing your skills.

THE SKILLS CHECKLIST

Refer to the following checklist as you write your resume to ensure that you are including the most sought-after qualities that hiring managers look for in resumes:

☐ Have I included all of my skills and are they truly reflective of the work I have done?

☐ Does my resume reflect a strong work ethic through examples of successes and accomplishments beyond my basic duties?

☐ Have I infused my resume with a sense of enthusiasm, or is it dry and dull?

☐ Is my resume written clearly and concisely? Is it free of errors?

☐ Does my resume indicate that I have good people skills and will work well with fellow employees?

☐ Is my resume truthful?

☐ Does my resume convey confidence? Does it steer clear of unsubstantiated claims?

☐ Have I organized the resume in a way that is easy to read and pleasing to the eye?

☐ Have I offered insight into my personality using words and examples?

☐ Have I included all the recent training and courses that I have taken?

CHAPTER SUMMARY

In this chapter, you learned 10 qualities that hiring managers look for when evaluating resumes and how to write those qualities into your resume.

CHAPTER 6

The Resume Heading

In this chapter, you learn how to write an effective resume heading that includes all the information a hiring manager will want. It also teaches you how to handle tricky issues that might arise as you write the heading.

HEADING FUNDAMENTALS

The heading is found at the top of the resume. It is the first thing the reader's eyes encounter as they begin to scan the page. It must be neat, orderly, accurate, and thorough.

Today's resume headings contain a lot more information than they used to. In the past, a resume heading typically contained little more than your name, address, and telephone number. A more modern resume is likely to include your e-mail address, your cell phone number, your beeper number, your voice mail, or even your fax number! If the hiring manager perceives you as being easy to reach, he or she is more likely to call you in for an interview. You also tend to look more business savvy if you include these communications options at the top of your resume.

The easier you are to reach, the more likely it is that a hiring manager will invite you for a job interview with the company.

Follow these rules for deciding whether or not to include information in your heading:

- Include a cell phone or beeper number only if this is your main source of communication throughout the day.
- Do not include an e-mail address if you do not check your e-mail regularly.
- Add a voice-mail number only if you have confidential access.
- Only include an e-mail address that has a professional tone. Leave it off or change it if it is cutesy or humorous.

Only include an e-mail address in the resume heading if you check your e-mail daily. Don't miss an interview offer because you forgot to read the e-mail!

Be careful not to clutter your heading with too many numbers. Two or three communications options ought to be plenty.

YOUR NAME

Writing your name at the top of the resume is a simple task for most folks. For others, it can be a tricky exercise in figuring out just what to include and how to choose the best name to use.

If you are not sure about the best way to present your name on your resume, follow these general rules:

- Always leave off the formal titles, Mr., Ms., and Mrs.
- Beware of using the surname "Senior" on your resume. It reveals some family statistics and might be better left off.
- It is better not to write out your full middle name on a resume, but to use the initial instead. Otherwise, the reader might be confused about how to address you. For example, is "Mary Patricia Bowles" addressed as "Mary Patricia" or simply "Mary"? However:
- If your name does not identify your gender (such as Terry or Chris), you might want to use your full middle name on the resume (for example, Terry Elizabeth Webster or Terry Alan Smith). This will reduce the feeling of uncertainty for the personnel representative, which makes him or her more likely to call you!
- You can include titles or degrees (such as Ph.D., CPA, LPN) after your name, especially if they relate to your career field and will be easily recognized and understood by your target audience. You worked hard to earn them, so flaunt them!
- If you are known by your middle name rather than your first name, write it using the first initial, such as J. Bradley Worthmore. You can also choose to leave off the first initial altogether.

The Use of Nicknames

A resume is not an official or legal document, so there is no law requiring you to use your birth name on a resume. The following are some points to consider:

- It is wise to steer clear of nicknames in most cases, to give your resume a more professional, polished appeal.
- If the nickname you plan to use is the name you use consistently in business and personal situations, you can use the nickname on the resume instead of your birth name (for example, "Stan" instead of "Stanley" or "Tom" instead of "Thomas").
- If the nickname is unusual, cutesy, humorous, or difficult to pronounce, don't use it.

  Example: A woman, whose actual name is Beulah, is known to her friends as "Boots." Because she doesn't like the name "Beulah" and because "Boots" is an unusual and informal name, she uses her middle name, "Anne," on her resume and in a business setting.

Example: Robert, a professional accountant for 18 years, is known informally among his friends and coworkers as "Bobby." Although "Bobby" is too informal a name to put on his resume, he did not want to stick with the very formal "Robert." Instead, he chose "Bob" as the happy medium for his name on the resume.

Question and Answer

Should I write an introduction, such as the word "resume" or "curriculum vitae," at the top of my resume?

No. Although this type of introduction was once routinely written as a standard heading for the resume, this is now considered passé.

Should I include my current work number on my resume?

It depends upon your situation at work. If you would be devastated to have your boss find out that you are seeking other employment, then it is better to play it safe and leave the work number off. If, however, your boss and coworkers are aware that you are looking for a new position, you are welcome to include it on your resume.

Will it be seen as a negative if I don't have a work number on my resume?

No. A personnel representative will assume that either you are keeping your job search confidential or you are unemployed. Years ago, a job seeker, who was unemployed, raised red flags with personnel because they were afraid of a bad work history. However, with the massive layoffs and corporate downsizings that dominate our business culture today, being unemployed while job seeking is no longer seen as a negative.

What if I am planning to change my address in the near future?

Because resumes can now be stored in computers and accessed easily for simple changes, it shouldn't be difficult to rewrite your address and phone number when you need to. Remember, however, that everyone you have given the old resume to will be unable to reach you once you've moved. The best scenario is to mark your resume with both current and future address and phone:

JOHN GOODWIN	After August 15
Prior to August 15	5700 McCarthy Court
1625 April Garth	Lakota, Ohio 45069
Lakota, Ohio 45069	(513) 291-0757

YOUR PHONE NUMBER

As you send out resumes with your phone number on them, be sure that you have an answering machine at home to pick up calls when you are away. A personnel representative might never try a second time to reach you if he or she has tried before and gotten no answer!

Be sure that your answering machine message is appropriate to the possibility of business calls. It must be brief and professional. This means:

- No kids talking or giggling
- No music, not even soft music, in the background
- No jokes, singing, or silliness
- No lengthy speeches or explanations

Your voice message should be simple and succinct, such as:

> "Hi. You've reached 456-7789. Please leave a message, and I'll return your call as soon as possible."

 Do not name all of the people in your family on the message ("Hi. You've reached Bill, Kathy, Sandy, Bobby, and Baby Jake!" This reveals your family statistics, which might not translate favorably to a potential employer.

After your job search is over, you can change your message back to include whatever you prefer. For now, however, the rule is *simple* and *professional*.

DESIGNING YOUR HEADING

Heading Placement

Your resume's heading can be located along the right margin, the left margin, centered on the page, or divided into two columns. It should be clearly written and easy to read.

The three rules to remember for the heading are that it should be
1. Clear
2. Correct
3. Complete

Right Margin

Many experts argue that a right-margin heading is the best placement because it is the easiest to read if the hiring manager places the resume in an employment binder.

SALLY CAMPBELL
5757 Ocello Drive
Chester, MA 54565
(401) 555-6878

Left Margin

A left-margin placement makes sense because we read from left to right, and so the heading begins the resume page. This also has the familiar feel of a business letter format.

SALLY CAMPBELL
5757 Ocello Drive
Chester, MA 54565
(410) 555-6878

Centered

A centered resume heading can be the most visually pleasing.

SALLY CAMPBELL
5757 Ocello Drive
Chester, MA 54565
(410) 555-6878

Columns

It can be best to divide a heading into columns or lines if the heading is lengthy and you are in need of space. Beware of overloading the columns, or you might end up with a confusing or cluttered look.

SALLY CAMPBELL

5757 Ocello Drive   Chester, MA 54565   (410) 555-6878

Use a font that gives your resume a professional tone, such as Courier or Arial. Don't use a whimsical, script, or shadowed font that might be difficult to read.

 How to place the resume heading is a matter of your own choice. There is no one correct placement for a resume heading.

Visual Techniques

To set your heading apart from the body of the resume, you can use special visual techniques to capture the reader's eye. Try one of these options:

- Larger font
- Bold typeface
- Underlined name
- Italicized name
- Different ink color on name
- Heading separated from resume by bold line
- The name in all capital letters

Examples:

James Dougherty
5116 Winchester Road
Questfield, Oregon 16789

JAMES DOUGHERTY
5116 Winchester Road
Questfield, Oregon 16789

James Dougherty
5116 Winchester Road
Questfield, Oregon 16789

JAMES DOUGHERTY
5116 Winchester Road
Questfield, Oregon 16789

 Do not get overly elaborate with these visual techniques in your resume heading. You will want to call attention to many more areas on the resume, and too many frills in the heading will continually distract the reader's eye.

WORKSHOP

Fill in your personal information below:

Name:_____

Address:_____

City/state/zip:_____

Phone:_____

Cell/beeper (optional): _____

E-mail (optional):_____

Voice Mail (optional):_____

Fax # (optional):_____

CHAPTER SUMMARY

In this chapter, you learned the keys to writing a resume heading that is pleasing to the eye, informative, and consistent with today's resume trends.

CHAPTER 7

The Summary Section

In this chapter, you will learn how to write a Summary section that reflects the highlights of your work experience and skills.

The Summary section of the resume is perhaps the most important section to work hard on and to write well. This is the make-or-break section—the part of the resume that is initially scanned. If your resume passes this initial inspection, it goes on for further review. If the Summary section fails to engage the reader, he or she might never go on to read the rest.

WHAT IS THE SUMMARY?

The summary (or profile—you can choose to call it either one) is a quick overview of your employment background and strongest skills. Use it to paint an attractive picture of your strengths so the reader is enticed to want to read further down the page to get to know more about you. The summary directly follows the heading of your resume, and it takes the place of the "OBJECTIVE," or "JOB OBJECTIVE," found on resumes in the past.

A well-written summary is:

- **Concise** A summary should offer only the brightest highlights in abbreviated form. Anything more will lose impact.

- **Focused** A summary is not effective if it doesn't present an accurate portrayal of your strengths. Each individual piece should fit together to form a unified whole.

- **Enticing** The summary must capture the reader's attention immediately. It will be scanned only briefly; therefore, it must be written in such a way as to draw the eye quickly to its key parts.

 Everything you write in your summary must be substantiated in the body of the resume. The summary gives the highlights; the rest of the resume gives the details!

Objective Versus Summary

Resumes used to require a section directly under the name that offered the reader a description of the writer's desired career direction or aspirations. An objective said something like

> OBJECTIVE: Desire a challenging and rewarding position utilizing my broad skills and experience in retail merchandising.

Or,

> JOB OBJECTIVE: To obtain a challenging position where I can effectively utilize my training and experience in administrative management.

As you can see from these examples, the focus of an objective was on how a company might help the resume writer achieve his or her career goals.

The focus of today's summary is the opposite of this. The focus of a summary is not how a company might help *you* but how *you* might help the *company*. It demonstrates to the employer how you might benefit the company with your skills, experience, and positive attitude.

Employers aren't overly concerned with who you want to be in the future. They want to know who you are right now and what you can do for them now. With a well-written summary, you no longer need an old-fashioned job objective.

THE PARTS OF A SUMMARY

The following is an example of a typical summary format:

SUMMARY: A successful senior marketing executive with over 14 years of progressively responsible experience in the healthcare industry. Diverse background in marketing, business development, and general management with profit-and-loss responsibility. Known for organizational skills, time lines, and the ability to keep a cool head under pressure. Expertise in:

• Strategic Planning	• Budget Development
• Product Management	• Joint Marketing Agreements
• New Product Introduction	• Project Coordination

The traditional summary is made up of several important pieces that fit together snugly to form the backbone of a well-written resume. Refer to the summary above as we examine the parts that make up a typical summary.

1. **The Section Title** You can title this section of the resume "Summary," "Profile," or you can leave it without a title at all. Others have labeled it "Executive Summary" or "Summary of Qualifications," but a shorter title creates more space and looks tidier.

2. **The First Words** Words like "successful," "dedicated," and "enthusiastic" offer the reader insight into your personal skills that make you a good choice to hire. Choose these from your list of intuitive skills that you identified in chapter 2.

3. **The First Sentence** The first sentence of the summary should be an attention-grabber that gets right to the heart of who you are and what your background is. It should include a well-thought-out title that gives your reader an immediate sense of who you are. You must find a descriptive title that is broad enough to keep you from being pigeonholed and yet is detailed enough to give your summary focus. This will probably not be any one actual job title you have held but a more inclusive term that combines your experience and packages it into a comprehensive term.

You must keep in mind your career goals as you formulate this new title. Look back at your job goals statement in chapter 3. What is your desired career as you write this resume? Take care to match your summary title to your job goals.

Take care to write a title that is *descriptive* but not *restrictive*.

Examples:

Summary titles that are too broad:

Corporate Executive

Business Professional

Management Professional

Industry Leader

These titles do not define the applicant enough to provide the reader with any information about the writer.

Summary titles that are too narrow:

City Desk Clerk II

Vice President, Information Systems

Second-Shift Production Supervisor

Assistant Student Athletic Trainer

These titles do not define you broadly enough for the summary because they are specific to a single job title. They do not encompass a broader experience base. Even if your work experience involves only one position, you should still broaden the description to be more inclusive of your skills.

Summary titles that are just right:

Senior Personnel Administrator

Interior Design Professional

Office Support Specialist

Junior Marketing Executive

These titles tell the reader the field you are in and, perhaps, your level of expertise. They do not detail a particular position.

4. **Years of Experience**   After you have devised a title for yourself, calculate how many years you have been doing work in this field or a related field. You can choose to leave the specific number of years off this portion of the resume, but if you want to include your years of experience, as was done in the summary example, follow these rules:

   a. If you have fewer than five years of experience, it might be wise to use the words "several years experience," rather than the actual number. (This was done in the accomplishments summary above.) Alternatively, you might choose to use a different phrase, such as "broad experience," "a diverse background," or some other wording that does not call attention to a lack of experience in the field.

   b. If you have 5 to 20 years of experience, you can specify the number directly to alert the hiring manager to your ample work history.

   c. If you have more than 20 years of experience in the field, you might choose a phrase such as "extensive background," rather than pinpointing a number. This will protect you from possible age discrimination.

5. **The Industry**   You might want to identify the industry that you have been working in to give your resume greater focus. You might also choose to indicate program areas or other specifics that give the hiring manager a clearer picture of your background.

 Include the industry background only if you want to stay in the same (or a similar) industry. Otherwise, personnel representatives might worry that your skills won't transfer.

6. **Technical Skills**   The midsection of the summary gives you a chance to highlight a few broad technical skills that you have been using in recent positions. Choose them carefully. Remember that you want to paint just the right portrait of yourself, which will open doors to the career you are seeking.

7. **Intuitive Skills** Some resume writers prefer to add a sentence toward the end of the summary that emphasizes their intuitive skills. This adds a bit of personal interest to your resume and paints a more rounded picture of who you are and what you have to offer.

8. **The Close** At the end of the summary, add a short transitional sentence that moves you into the bulleted "learned" skills section of your summary. Use short phrases such as, "expertise in:" or "Background includes:" or "Special skills in:".

9. **The Bullets** The bulleted section of your summary should be a solid, defined list of six to eight skills that directly relate to the position for which you are applying or to your career field. They should not be nebulous, but they should be direct, specific skills that could transfer directly into a new position.

 The summary is the section of the resume that will attract the most attention. Because of its placement near the top of the page and the use of the bullets, most hiring managers read this section of the resume first.

SKILLS VERSUS ACCOMPLISHMENTS

The two most common types of summaries are the Skills Summary and the Accomplishments Summary. The Skills Summary, shown in the example on page 58, contains a bulleted list of six or more of your specific proven skills.

The top portion of an Accomplishments Summary (on the following page), is identical in form to the Skills Summary. Where it differs is in the bulleted list. Instead of focusing on specific skills, the Accomplishments Summary highlights particular quantified accomplishments that you have achieved in recent positions. In this type of summary, you will need a bulleted list of three to five specific activities with identifiable results. They should be brief powerful statements that prove you can deliver.

SUMMARY: Dedicated, enthusiastic physical education specialist with several years experience in corporate fitness/wellness programming. Diverse background with strong credentials in physical fitness, injury prevention, and health education. Known for creativity, tenacity, and the ability to motivate others. Accomplishments include:

- Received outstanding reviews for programs in exercise physiology, kinesiology, and motor learning from management teams in eight district offices.
- Introduced an Athletic Injuries Prevention program that reduced injuries at corporate facilities by 20 percent in the first year.
- Successfully created, implemented, and managed six corporate organized team athletic programs.

KEEPING THE OBJECTIVE

If you still feel that your resume is missing something without an objective at the top, you may include one. As I have said, there is no one standard format for resume writing, and there is certainly room to make it your own as you please. However, to be consistent with the resume format of today, an objective should be a simple title or brief statement of job goals.

Examples:

OBJECTIVE: Vice President of Sales and Marketing

OBJECTIVE: Rehabilitative Physical Therapist

If you do use an objective, be aware that you might unintentionally define yourself incorrectly for a particular company. For example, a resume marked "OBJECTIVE: Graphics Designer" might be directed toward a position in graphics design, whereas the job seeker would have been better suited for a job in the Graphic Arts department of the organization. In other words, a very definitive job objective can pigeonhole your resume in the wrong area simply because of a difference in semantics.

You must write your objective carefully to avoid confining your job prospects to one job title only.

QUESTIONS AND ANSWERS

What if I am not sure what my career direction should be?

In that case, it would be wise to return to chapter 3 and work on your job objective statement again. Summaries that are written without a clear career direction in mind lose much of their impact and dilute the power of the entire resume.

What if I just keep struggling with the summary and can't seem to get it right?

Many people have trouble writing the summary. A good solution is to try writing the rest of the resume first, and then return to write the summary when you are done with the rest. Sometimes writing the other sections helps you focus in on your skills and background with a new perspective.

It is difficult for me to summarize my experience because I have just graduated from school and I don't have much experience to summarize!

No problem. Just shorten the summary a bit and spend more time highlighting your intuitive skills rather than worrying about the learned skills you might lack. Remember that intuitive skills are what set the good resumes apart from the mediocre ones.

WORKSHOP

Use one of the following templates to craft your unique summary. Add your own creativity to fashion a summary that reflects your brightest highlights.

Use your intuitive and learned skills lists that you developed in chapter 2 to complete your summary.

(I.S.) = Intuitive skill

(L.S.) = Learned skill

Template 1

_____ (I.S.), _____ (I.S) _____
_____ (Summary title) with over_____(Number)
years in the _____ industry. Broad background in _____
_____ (L.S.), _____ (L.S.), and _____ (L.S.).
Known for _____ (I.S.) and _____ (I.S.).
Particular expertise in

-
-
-
-

Template 2

_____ (I.S.) _____ (industry) professional
with expertise in _____ (L.S.) and _____
(L.S.). Extensive background in _____ (L.S.) and
_____ (L.S.) Widely recognized for _____
(I.S.), _____ (I.S.), and _____ (I.S.).
Particular accomplishments include:

-
-
-
-

CHAPTER SUMMARY

In this chapter, you learned how to write a powerful and focused summary
that highlights your skills and experience.

CHAPTER 8

The Experience Section

In this chapter, you learn to masterfully sum-
marize your professional history in the main
body of the resume. You will learn the eight
keys to a great Experience section, and how to
sell your skills to the resume reader.

The Experience section is the most information-packed portion of the resume. It gives the potential employer a wide-angle portrait of your work history in recent years—a substantial record of where you've been, what you've been doing, and most importantly, how well you've been doing it.

This section of the resume is handled differently depending on whether the resume is written in the functional or chronological format. The functional format places little emphasis on the Experience section of the resume, whereas the chronological format devotes the bulk of its space to work experience. For this reason, we will concentrate our discussion on the chronological format in this chapter.

THE EXPERIENCE SECTION, IN DEPTH

The chronological resume lists your current and previous positions in reverse chronological order. This means you start with the most recent position you held, and then work backwards in time from there. This allows the reader to track your job history from your latest position back to your earliest.

 Do not stray from the reverse chronological format. It will confuse personnel representatives who expect to see a last-to-first presentation of work history.

The Experience section usually takes up the bulk of a chronological resume page, whether the writer has had two years of experience or twenty. Each position you have held should include these 5 basic bits of information:

1. The name and location of the company

2. The dates that you worked for the company

3. Your job title(s)

4. A description of your duties

5. Your accomplishments beyond your basic duties

The Name and Location of the Company

Each organization you have worked for should be listed with full company name and the city and state where it is located. For example:

EMPLOYMENT HISTORY

1985–1996   Midtown General Hospital   Chicago, IL

 A full street address is not necessary for each company; the city and state are sufficient.

If you worked at several locations of the same company throughout the year because of job requirements or relocation, you can identify the location you worked with each position title you describe, or you can list the locations as in the following examples:

| DUNCRAFT & SCHMIDT | 1994–1998 |
| Fremont, AZ and Kings, NM | |

WILSON ELECTRONICS	1987–1999
Ferndale, MS	(1987–1991)
Glenmore, IA	(1992–1999)

Some resume writers worry that they will confuse the reader if the location in which they worked is just a small satellite office of a large corporate headquarters. In this case, it is best to cite the location where you reported to work each day, rather than the headquarters location.

What Companies Should I Include?

It is not necessary to detail each position you have held throughout your employment history. You can eliminate early positions that do not relate to your current job goals, or you can give them a brief notice without much detail.

If you are a recent high school or college graduate with little pertinent work experience, however, you can include minimum wage work on the resume to indicate employment credibility.

Eliminate minimum wage entry-level jobs that you held while attending high school or college from your resume if you have had more than three years of successful employment beyond this work.

As a general rule, include all positions that you have held for more than six months in the last 10–15 years.

If the firm is a subsidiary of a larger organization, indicate the name of the parent company as well. The more name recognition the better!

A Description of the Company

Some resume writers prefer to add a description of the products the firm manufactures or the service it performs. They place this directly under or beside the name of the organization. This gives the resume reader some idea what kind of business it is.

Examples:

MAKINO, INC.   Cincinnati, OH   1996–Present

World leading machine tool manufacturer for aerospace industry.

or

BRIGHT ASSOCIATES   Orange, New Jersey   (1982–1994)

(Largest Executive Recruiting firm in East Coast Region)

 Adding a description of the firm is a luxury, not a necessity. If you are short on space, you can leave it off. If you are looking for filler, keep it in!

The Dates that You Worked for the Company

It is no longer necessary to detail the specific months of employment. On today's resume, simply write the years that you worked for an organization, as in the examples above. Include the year that you started with them and the year that your employment ended, or you can state "Present" if you still work there, as in "1995–Present."

 If you worked for an organization only one year, write that year alone, as in "1997," rather than, "1997–1997."

A Gap in Employment History

If you have a large gap in your employment history, personnel representatives are likely to notice this. Because of the tumultuous state of today's work world, gaps of six months to a year are no longer seen as the negative they once were. A period of unemployment lasting longer than one year, however, is likely to raise the resume reader's concern.

 Remember, no matter how reasonable your explanation for this period of unemployment, you will not get a chance to defend yourself if you never make it into the interview. Your resume must make the hiring manager feel that you are a good hiring risk.

The best way to tackle this problem is to leave nothing to chance. If you have a reasonable explanation for a gap in employment, such as a return to school or a period of overseas travel, you might choose to clarify it right on the resume. For example:

CLARIFORM U.S.A.	Morgantown, WV	1992–1995
FULL-TIME STUDENT	Petersburg, WV	1990–1992

Returned to school to earn master's degree in structural engineering.

PRECISION DIECASTERS	Trenton, OH	1986–1990

You might also use any intermittent professional work you did during this time, whether paid or unpaid, as your "job experience."

There is no need to delve into the details of your studies, travels, or other aspects of your unemployed time. You want to fill in the gap, but you don't want to waste precious space in the Experience section of the resume. You might decide to elaborate in the Education or Other section of the resume.

Lengthy Unemployment

If you have had difficulty locating a new job during an extended period and have nothing to fill in the date gap, don't fret needlessly over something you can't change. Simply write your work experience and your dates of employment truthfully and accurately.

In a section toward the bottom of the resume, such as "Education," "Additional Courses," or "Other," it would be wise to indicate any activity that you pursued during your period of unemployment. State, for example, any courses you might have taken at a community college to sharpen your skills or any volunteer work you did for a local organization. This tells the employer that you were an active member of the community during your unemployment and that you kept your skills sharp and your attitude positive.

Your Job Title

After the name of the firm and the dates you were employed, write your most recent job title, followed by any previous titles held.

You might need to add to your resume the dates during which you held each title, as in:

WOKMAN, INC.	Philadelphia, PA	(1984–1992)
Programming Analyst		(1990–1992)
Programmer		(1987–1990)
Data Processor		(1984–1987)

This demonstrates your progression within the organization and paints you as a valuable, productive employee.

 In some cases, it is best to clarify your title by adding the division or group you were associated with, such as *Group Manager, Consumer Products Division.*

You might choose to provide details about each position separately (see the resumes on page 131). If the positions you held had very similar responsibilities, however, you can choose to write one overall job description that encompasses all of your positions (see the resumes on pages 130 and 183–184).

If you do not have an official job title, you must provide one that is accurate and realistic. Give yourself a title that is reflective of the work you did.

Don't exaggerate your responsibilities in the job title. If your potential employer calls a previous employer for references, you don't want to appear dishonest.

 Do not write a job description without including a job title. This will confuse personnel representatives who are scanning the resume for titles, and might cause confusion or raise suspicions.

A Description of Your Duties

The Experience section of the resume has changed dramatically over the past several years. It is no longer the detailed listing of job responsibilities that it was in the past. No longer is the focus on what duties your past jobs required, but on how well *you personally* fulfilled those requirements.

When writing a description of your duties, remember this: An employer does not need to see every job responsibility you had in each position that you've held. Instead, he or she wants to see the skills and qualities that *you* brought to the job. Employers want to see proof that you were good at what you did.

 Employers know that the best indicator of how well someone will work at a new job is not *what* they did in the past, but *how well they did it.*

Continue with this pattern of company name, title, job description, and dates of employment back through your career, usually going back no more than about 15 years. The farther back in time you go, the briefer the position description. You might also choose to list early positions by company and title alone, omitting a position description altogether.

Employers are interested in these early positions mainly to get a feel for how your career has progressed and with which organizations you have been involved.

Your Accomplishments

The accomplishments that you identify under each position description are perhaps the most important part of the Experience section. They tell the potential employer that you are a successful employee who knows how to achieve results.

The accomplishments portion of your Experience section will be discussed in chapter 9.

FORMATTING THE EXPERIENCE SECTION

Your experience should be written in block paragraph form directly under or beside the job title. Each job you describe should be set up exactly as the others so that there is a predictable flow to the resume, which makes it easier to read. Concentrate on the three Cs:

1. **Cohesive**   Remember to draw upon your lists of learned and intuitive skills as you write your experience. Are you demonstrating these skills through your description and your use of examples? A well-written resume paints a unified portrait of you with a specific skill set and a clear career focus.

2. **Consistent**   Keep all margins, indentations, and formatting consistent with each position you describe. Match those verb tenses, too!

3. **Concise**   The most powerful resumes use hard-hitting words that are not diluted by unnecessary information or lengthy phrasing.

Many resume writers complain that they have too much to say to be able to fit everything into the short space a resume allows. Yet, I have seen top-level managers fit 30 years of complex experience expertly onto two pages. I've seen the opposite of this, too: entry level workers with less than five years of experience sprawling onto four pages of resume space.

Keep your description of job duties to no more than four or five sentences. A two- or three-sentence description is even better.

The Experience section must be written in a concise, efficient format. Be very careful to extract unnecessary words or phrases and delete them entirely so that what is left is clear and crisp. For example:

BEFORE (wordy):

"Answered letters in regard to complaints by writing adjustment letters."

AFTER (concise):

"Wrote adjustment letters to answer complaints."

BEFORE (wordy):

Reconcilement Specialist

Updated new information into reconcilement reports on a daily basis. Produced a new report every week and at month-end. Worked with various intercompany departments to settle all general ledger accounts. Conducted research on account differences, and corrected those differences when necessary. Responsible for coordinating all accounts with customers inside and outside the company.

AFTER (concise):

Reconcilement Specialist

Produced and maintained reconcilement reports on a daily, weekly, and monthly basis. Settled general ledger accounts with intercompany departments. Researched and corrected account differences, and coordinated accounts with internal and external customers.

EIGHT KEYS TO A GREAT EXPERIENCE SECTION

1. **Use short, telegraphic phrases**   There is no need to write complete sentences on a resume. Throw everything you learned in grammar class out the window. Punctuate each phrase like a sentence, however, regardless of whether it truly qualifies as a sentence.

2. **Avoid the use of "I" on the resume**   An occasional use of the word "I" is acceptable, but using it in every instance would be overpowering on the resume. Resume readers will assume that you are the implied subject.

3. **Do not use the phrase "Responsible for"**   This dilutes the power of your message by putting everything in a passive tense. All it says is what you were *supposed* to do, but did you really do it?

4. **Use action verbs that end in "–ed," especially at the start of sentences**   Action verbs send the strongest message that you accomplished things on the job. Words like *initiated, created, improved,* and *directed* sound active and powerful.

5. **Emphasize results**   Employers are not concerned so much about how hard you worked, as they are about how *well* you worked. How effective were you in the tasks you were given? Did you save the company time or money? If so, how?

6. **Quantify**   Always make use of numbers and figures to give your resume a hard-facts feel. The less nebulous it is, the better. Give specific numbers on how many employees you supervised, how many phone lines you answered, how many customers you dealt with each day, week, or month, how many contracts you serviced per quarter, and so on.

7. **Less is more**   Take out all extra words, especially any unnecessary "a" or "the" you've used.

8. **Avoid vague words and phrases, such as "handled" or "worked on"**   Write your resume as if the reader had no idea what your job involved, because chances are, he or she won't. If you say, "Handled workers compensation claims," what does that mean exactly? Did you file them, type them, distribute them, or make decisions on them? Be clear and specific.

Experience Section Dos and Don'ts

DO use bullets to draw the eye to the most important part of your Experience section—your accomplishments.

DON'T overuse self-serving inflating words, such as "dynamic," "brilliant," or "innovative."

DO keep the format cohesive, concise, and consistent.

DON'T use shoptalk or technical jargon. Translate all terms into general business terms.

DO use concrete, specific nouns and verbs, which provide a tone of motivation and confidence.

DON'T include names of bosses or telephone numbers of former employers.

DO remain positive throughout. There is no reason for anything negative on the resume at any time! Avoid words like "no," "not," "lack," and "never."

DON'T explain why you left a job. Whether it was for a positive or a negative reason, do not include it on your resume.

CHAPTER SUMMARY

In this chapter, you learned to write an Experience section that effectively sells your skills to an employer.

CHAPTER 9

Use Accomplishments to Prove Your Case

In this chapter, you learn to highlight your accomplishments on your resume to create a dynamic emphasis on your successes.

HOW TO USE ACCOMPLISHMENTS

Just as it is important to give an employer a picture of your work history through carefully chosen examples of your most noteworthy responsibilities, it is equally important to engage the employer's imagination with a sampling of your most outstanding achievements over the years.

No employer gets excited over a dry, lengthy paragraph full of job duties and tasks performed. You need to bring life to your work history by giving it a personal touch: What did YOU do to make a difference?

The accomplishments you choose will play a big part in how the resume reader envisions you. He or she will be searching them not only for job-related skills but for your intuitive skills as well: those that are a part of your personality and help spell success on the job. Take care to choose your accomplishments carefully, and to write them in a way that makes them stand out.

You already learned what an accomplishment is from Chapter 2, "Know Your Accomplishments and Skills," and you might even be able to incorporate some of the accomplishments you wrote in chapter 2 directly into your resume. Chances are, however, you will have to develop other accomplishments to make your resume balanced and complete.

ACCOMPLISHMENTS AT WORK

Many resume writers fret that nothing in their entire work history qualifies as an outstanding accomplishment. "I just went to work every day and did the best that I could," is the typical comment. This couldn't be more wrong. Anyone who has put in a hard day's work in a job for more than a year or two has enough accomplishments to fill up 10 resumes. The trick is in identifying those accomplishments.

Think of the things that you did well that someone else might not have done as creatively. How did you put a little extra into a job when you might have gotten away with less? Identify specific examples that prove your worth to a potential employer.

Maybe it was an efficiency problem at work. Did you ever realign a process to make things run more quickly or more effectively? Maybe it was a key contract you landed or a hard-to-please customer you won over. Could it have been a project you coordinated without a hitch? A tough deadline you met or even beat? Something new you designed? A room full of people you taught or trained? A system you reorganized? Maybe it was simply that you were unusually reliable. Your employer could count on you to be there and to get the job done every day, come what may.

Think of all the ways that you brought more to the job than was written in the requirements because of a great idea or special talent you had. These are the makings of accomplishments!

Follow these general rules to write your accomplishments:

1. Each recent position you describe in your Experience section should have at least three bulleted accomplishments, which directly follow the description of job duties.

2. Each accomplishment should be written in one to three lines, and should be a specific task or problem that you handled successfully.

3. It is important to state not only the achievement itself but also the *results* of that achievement.

4. The only times you might choose not to pinpoint specific accomplishments after a job description is when:

   - You held the job more than 15 years ago.

   - The job you are describing is preceded by at least three other jobs, all of which have included a list of accomplishments.

 The farther back in time you go, the less need there is to specify accomplishments on the job.

5. Choose accomplishments that highlight the skills that apply to the career you are seeking.

6. Never let a single accomplishment stand alone after the description of duties for a position. This can look weaker than having none at all.

7. Do not list more than six accomplishments under one position description.

Examples of the Experience Section with Accomplishments

Kore-Walker, Inc.   Forestville, IN   1991–1998

Global Sourcing Manager

Coordinated international procurement operations to support North/South American spare-part requirements. Supported 54 product lines.

- Initiated and conducted sourcing activities with Kore-Walker's German, Swiss, Asian, and U.S. operations. Dealt effectively across cultural lines.

- Created and coordinated Supplier Certification Program, which accurately measured performance of 400+ suppliers.

- Established an internal networking system for six regional warehouses across the U.S. and Mexico, which increased support to strategic customers by expediting zone-to-zone communication.

Notice that the accomplishments she chose to highlight are not mere job duties but specific examples of particular successes or improved operations.

 A common mistake in resume writing is to single out everyday job duties and bullet them as special accomplishments. This mutes the impact of the actual accomplishments you've highlighted and confuses the description of your skills.

EVERYDAY ACCOMPLISHMENTS

If you are still having trouble developing a list of outstanding accomplishments, try using creative wording to accent your daily duties.

Sometimes it helps to examine the tasks you completed on a daily basis and analyze your effectiveness. It is possible to turn a daily duty into an outstanding accomplishment through careful phrasing. Instead of sounding bored about the work you did, make yourself sound conscientious and proud.

For example:

"Answered phones for various departments." (A daily duty)

"Managed incoming calls for five busy departments on 15-line phone system. Always dealt courteously and professionally with current clients and new inquiry calls." (An accomplishment)

"Contacted delinquent loan accounts and recommended appropriate action to resolve default." (A daily duty)

"Consistently met and exceeded daily activity requirements for delinquent account phone calls and account resolution." (An accomplishment)

"Processed paperwork and maintained records." (A daily duty)

"Accurately processed paperwork and maintained records for over 200 industrial supply orders per week." (An accomplishment)

Another way to turn daily duties into proud accomplishments is to focus on the *results* of your work. How did your efforts save the company time or money?

For example:

"Developed incentive programs to motivate personnel." (A daily duty)

"Developed incentive programs that rewarded personnel and motivated them to achieve a 40 percent increase in production in a single year." (A proud accomplishment)

"Maintained company financial statements." (A daily duty)

"Maintained financial statement ratios at an acceptable level, which preserved company's A.M. Best rating." (A proud accomplishment)

 After you've created your list of accomplishments, prioritize them within each job description so that the most impressive ones come first!

WORKSHOP

As you write each accomplishment, follow these basic guidelines:

Start with an action verb.

Example: Initiated, Created, Implemented, Coordinated.

Add descriptive words when necessary to add spice to your action verbs.

Example: "Maintained"

becomes,

"consistently maintained";

"Reviewed"

becomes,

"thoroughly reviewed."

Quantify whenever possible.

Example: "Dealt with customers,"

becomes,

"Dealt with 40+ customers daily."

Finish with results.

Example: "Devised inventory control system"

becomes,

"Devised inventory control system, which improved efficiency of warehouse operations."

CHAPTER SUMMARY

In this chapter, you learned how to write accomplishments that highlight your skills by focusing on concrete examples of past successes.

CHAPTER 10

The Education Section

In this chapter, you learn to recognize what hiring managers look for in a resume's Education section and how to write yours to impress the reader.

WHY HAVE AN EDUCATION SECTION?

The story is the same across all chronological resume formats: No matter whether you have a Ph.D., an A.A. degree, or a G.E.D., your academic history must be displayed on your resume in its own prominent section.

"Why would someone care about the high school diploma that I earned 20 years ago?" some job seekers ask. The answers vary.

In some instances, educational level is a major qualifier for the job. You've seen the job ads: "Applicant must have bachelor's degree in chemistry or biochemistry."

Other position requirements are more flexible. Hiring managers are interested in seeing the educational level that you've achieved, but they are most interested in the job skills that you've acquired in recent years.

In either case, the more information an employer has about you, the more comfortable he or she feels about the risk of hiring you.

A resume that does not include an Education section is universally considered incomplete.

HOW HIRING MANAGERS REVIEW YOUR EDUCATION

Some hiring managers will be following a rigid checklist of the qualifications necessary to meet the job requirements. During the initial screening of the resume, the task is to weed out any unqualified applicants who don't meet the basic standards of the job at hand. Often, this involves a minimum educational requirement.

Their checklist is usually divided into different levels of educational achievement:

Less than high school diploma

G.E.D. (General Educational Development)

High school diploma

Some college work

Associate's degree (Two yr. college)

Two-year degree, some coursework beyond

Bachelor's degree (Four yr. college)

Four-year degree, plus some coursework

Master's degree

Ph.D. (Doctor of Philosophy)

Other (Professional school, etc.)

In some employment situations, such as government work, the salary you receive will be directly reflective of the level of education you have earned.

In other cases, your educational level does not directly affect your salary, but it might reflect the level of position you will be considered for. The higher the education level, the higher the position for which you will be considered.

THE EDUCATION SECTION FOR RECENT GRADUATES

Recent graduates with little professional experience must take careful time to write a creative and complete Education section of their resume, because this is the portion that will draw the keenest interest from employment managers.

What Employers Look For

If you have recently graduated from high school or college, and have little professional experience, employment managers will be basing a large part of their hiring decision on your educational background. They will be asking these questions as they review your resume:

- What was the applicant's field of study, and does it relate to the position we have available?
- Did the applicant have a solid, successful academic record?
- Did the applicant participate in outside activities during school?
- Did the applicant hold any positions of leadership during school?
- Was the applicant holding a job while he or she attended school?
- Did the job held while in school prepare him or her to work in a professional organization after graduation?

As a recent graduate, you might choose to expand upon your Education section to be sure that you include information that answers all of these important questions.

Four Tips for Recent Graduates

1. If you held a job during school that was an internship in a professional environment that relates to the career you are seeking, include details of this internship in the Experience section as if it were a full-time, salaried position.

2. If you worked in a job during your schooling that earned money but did not increase your professional skills, you should include it on your resume to indicate employability, but do not delve deeply into job details.

3. Be sure to include all activities you were involved in during your schooling. Even such activities as cheerleading, sports, or drama translate well into business skills. They indicate perseverance, a willingness to make decisions and take risks, and the ability to work as part of a team. They can be included in the Education section, or in a later section called, "Activities," or "Community Involvement."

4. If you are short on professional experience and long on resume space, you can detail school leadership experiences as if they were job experiences. For example, instead of simply saying, "President of Lakota Student Association," you can detail your responsibilities:

PRESIDENT OF STUDENT ASSOCIATION

LAKOTA HIGH SCHOOL 1998–1999

Represented student population on all school-related academic and recreational issues. Acted as liaison with school staff and faculty to foster stronger relationships and increased understanding of needs and expectations. Coordinated activities involving both staff and students.

- Created the annual "Fall Ball" event. Recruited and coordinated 25 volunteers to assist in planning and implementation. Designed task teams to oversee portions of the project. "Fall Ball" came in under budget and was attended by nearly 250 students.

- Coordinated monthly meetings with principal and vice principal to address student concerns and foster ongoing communications between decision-makers and students.

- Designed and cowrote biweekly student newsletter with a distribution of nearly 600 students and staff. Communicated with leaders of 18 school organizations to ensure timely submission of news and updates.

More Education Section Samples

1. **For high school graduate with some college work, but no degree:**

   Bradford College, Pittsburgh, PA (1998–1999)

   > Coursework in business and industrial relations

   Or,

   International Business College, Fort Wayne, IN (1992–1993)

   > Secretarial Sciences

2. **For Master's degree candidate:**

   M.S. Human Resource Administration, OHIO UNIVERSITY

   > (expected June, 2000)

   B.S. Psychology, MIAMI UNIVERSITY (1984)

3. **For technical school graduate:**

   Ivy Technical School, Atlanta, GA
   CAD Engineering Certificate (1998)

4. **For G.E.D.:**

   Columbus High School, Columbus, IN G.E.D. (1999)

5. **For Ph.D.:**

   Ph.D., ECONOMICS Graduate School of Business Administration, Metropolitan University, New York (1997)

   M.A., ECONOMICS Graduate School of Arts and Sciences, Metropolitan University, New York (1994)

   B.A., MATHEMATICS University of South Carolina (1990), Cum Laude

FORMATTING THE EDUCATION SECTION

Examine the two following sample Education sections and note how each offers complete information on your academic background without including details on specific classes you attended.

EDUCATION:

M.B.A., Finance, University of West Virginia, 1988

B.S., Business Administration, Northland College, 1974
Cum Laude

EDUCATION:

BROWN UNIVERSITY (1995)

B.A. Mathematics, minor Physics

UNIVERSITY OF PENNSYLVANIA (1996–1997)

Wharton Management Program

Where to Place Your Education Section

Most employers expect to find your education in one of two places on the resume: toward the end or toward the beginning.

If you have more than three years of professional work experience, your Education section should be placed toward the end of your resume. The more experience you have in the professional world, the less important your educational background becomes to the employer. Your years of experience take precedence over your years of schooling; therefore, your Education section should be placed after your Experience section.

If you have less than three years of professional experience, your Education section should be placed toward the beginning of the resume, directly under the summary. The less experience you have, the more a resume reader must rely upon your educational background to learn about you. Keep it toward the top, where it can be easily found and reviewed.

Guidelines to a Good Education Section

Although every Education section is unique, the traditional format is set up something like this:

Begin with Your Highest Degree Earned

Your highest completed degree should appear at the top of the Education section, with lesser degrees following. Two exceptions:

1. If you are currently pursuing a higher degree and are nearing completion of that degree, you can list your expected degree first.

2. If your highest degree is a high school diploma but you have taken some college courses, you can list those courses first.

If you have earned any type of college degree, do not list your high school diploma on your resume. Even if you have not earned a college degree, but have taken courses beyond the high school level at an institution that requires a high school diploma, do not list your high school education on the resume. Your diploma will be implied.

If you have earned a bachelor's degree, do not list an associate's degree that applied toward the higher degree, even if it was earned at a different school.

State the Name of Your School

There is no need to include a school address, or even the city and state in which it is located. However, you might choose to include city and state location for a small, local school that would not be recognized by the resume reader.

If the college you attended has an outstanding reputation or a highly recognizable name, indicate the school name boldly by placing it first, or using bold or all-capital letters.

State Your Date of Graduation

Do not include months. Simply write the year that you received your degree. Be careful not to include both start and end dates—these can lead the reader to mistakenly assume that you did not receive a degree!

If you didn't graduate from a program but attended courses at a school, however, you should include both start and end dates. You might also want to indicate your general course of study.

Please note that it is not necessary to include your date(s) of graduation or school attendance. You might prefer to leave the dates off if you graduated more than 20 years ago and if you are concerned that your skills might appear rusty or that you will face age discrimination.

State the Degree Earned and the Field of Study

Indicate your degree, followed by the field of study, especially if you earned your degree in a field directly related to your career field.

If your degree does not coincide with your current career direction (for example, your degree was in theater management but you are applying for a finance position), it is wise to leave off the course of study and simply state the degree itself, as in: B.A., University of Cincinnati 1996.

Do not write a long list of the individual college courses that you have taken toward your degree, unless you have earned a technical degree and have taken classes to develop particular hands-on skills the employer might be looking for.

Include your minor course of study only if it relates to your career goals.

Do not list seminars, workshops, or company-sponsored courses with your formal education unless you are short on copy. If you have attended more than one or two professional courses, it is best to give them their own section.

If your college coursework earned you a certificate rather than a degree, present it in the same way that you would a degree program.

 If you earned a generalized degree, but have a concentration in your career field, you can list this as: BA, PSYCHOLOGY (Industrial Relations) 1992.

Indicate Honors or Awards Achieved

Include academic honors and/or high grade point averages. Include your entire list of honors if you are a recent graduate. If you have more than five years of professional experience, list only the top two or three honors. If you graduated with honors, such as cum laude, magna cum laude, and so on, include this on your resume. Also include honorary academic organizations, such as Phi Beta Kappa or National Honor Society.

 You should not list the extracurricular school activities you participated in unless you are a recent graduate with less than three years of professional work experience.

WORKSHOP

Education Templates

Fill in the information on the template to develop your educational information.

Name of school where you earned your highest degree:

_____

_____

_____

Degree(s) earned, and field of study:

_____

_____

_____

If no degree, identify coursework:

_____

_____

_____

Date of graduation:

_____

_____

_____

Honors, awards, or G.P.A.:

_____

_____

_____

Name of school where next-highest degree was earned (or other courses taken):

_____

_____

_____

Degree earned, and field of study:

_____

_____

_____

If no degree, identify coursework:

_____

_____

_____

Date of graduation (or dates of attendance, if no degree):

_____

_____

_____

Honors, awards, or G.P.A.:

_____

_____

_____

CHAPTER SUMMARY

In this chapter, you learned what to include in your Education section and how to fit it to your individual needs.

CHAPTER 11

Creative Sections

In this chapter, you learn to invent your own creative sections to include all the information you want to appear on your resume.

YOUR UNIQUE RESUME

So far, we know that a resume must include four sections:

1. **Heading** Includes your name, address, and phone number.

2. **Summary** Highlights your greatest skills and puts them right at the top of the resume.

3. **Experience** Provides information on your past positions and particular accomplishments.

4. **Education** Gives the employer insight into your academic history.

But what about all those other things you want to talk about that don't fit into those four sections? Do you just have to leave it off and forget it?

Definitely not! This is your chance to get creative and structure your resume to include all the unique and positive traits that make you a great choice for any employer to hire.

CREATIVE SECTIONS THAT SAY IT ALL

You are now entering uncharted waters on your resume-writing journey. Up to this point, you've been following standard resume formatting and using guidelines that allow you to plug information into well-defined slots.

Now, however, some creative thinking is required. Let's examine the possibilities for adding a unique flavor to your resume by including creative sections.

Here are some suggestions for ways to categorize your leftover "stuff."

Technical Skills

Many of today's resume writers prefer to highlight their technical skills in a prominent section of their resume where they hope it will capture the attention of the hiring manager. These can be computer skills, office skills, or other clearly defined, hands-on skills that relate to the career you are seeking. You have three options for the Technical Skills section:

1. Don't include a Technical Skills section at all if you don't have more than two particular skills you want to highlight.

2. Place the Technical Skills section toward the end of the resume where it will be noticed, but might not receive immediate attention. This is a good idea if your technical skills are important to the job but not the make-or-break hiring factor.

3. Put the Technical Skills section right up front, just under the summary, if you feel your technical skills are the key aspect to landing the job you want (see the resumes on pages 110, 112, 113, 122, 123, and 133 for Technical Skills sections).

Examples:

TECHNICAL SKILLS: Industrial robotics, vibration analysis/laser alignment, pneumatics, hydraulics, statistical process control

TECHNICAL SKILLS: • System Configuration

• Fixed Disk Physical Format

• System Security

• Troubleshooting

Courses and Training

It is important to show that you are maintaining your skills and expanding upon others by taking courses and training sponsored by your present company. List all courses relevant to your general business skills or your particular career goals.

Community Activities

A current trend in employment today is to search for employees who are active members of the larger community. A person who is connected outside of the basic workday structure is considered healthy and friendly and perhaps less of a risk for burnout or short-term employment.

Include a section called "Community Activities," "Activities," "Volunteer Experience," or a similar title if you feel that you have the kind of community experience that can capture the attention of a potential employer.

If your community work shows off your leadership skills, organizational capabilities, or hardworking attitude, be sure it gets on the resume.

 Don't write a separate section for community activities if you have only one that you would like to include. Include a single community activity in another section of the resume.

Be careful to avoid listing any affiliations that might cause bad vibes in someone reading them. Even the most mainstream, mundane organizations might rub someone the wrong way. Avoid these topics:

- **Religion** Because religion is a touchy topic that makes personnel representatives squirm, some experts recommend leaving church volunteer work off of the resume altogether. If you feel that it is important to include it despite the risks, refrain from mentioning the denomination of the church you are affiliated with. For example, it is better to say, "taught Sunday School for 12 fourth graders," than it is to say, "taught Sunday School for 12 fourth graders at Lord of Life A.M.E. Church," or, "taught Catholic Youth Organization classes."

- **Politics** You might have played a big part in the Young
  Republicans Club local fundraising events, but watch out for those
  staunch Democrats who might be reading your resume. If you
  worked hard for a political organization and are reluctant to leave it
  off your resume, you might include the experience without including
  the political persuasion of the group. For example, don't say,
  "Exceeded fundraising goals by collecting $5K in contributions for
  campaign of Democratic senator Paul Serbont." Instead, say,
  "Exceeded fundraising goals by collecting $5K in contributions for
  senatorial political campaign."

- **Controversial Clubs** You are taking a chance of turning a potential employer completely off if you include such controversial organizations as the NRA, the ACLU, Planned Parenthood, NOW, or any
  groups that have a reputation for extreme tactics, like PETA or
  EarthFirst!. This is not to say you shouldn't belong to any of these
  groups; just don't put them on your resume.

- **Your Lifestyle** Before including information on community organizations to which you belong, think about what this will reveal to the
  resume reader. Writing that you are president of the local Parents
  Without Partners group tells the reader that you are either widowed
  or divorced and have children. They might see this as a hiring risk.
  Belonging to the school PTA also reveals your parent status. Leading
  a Brownie troop or coaching a peewee soccer team suggests young
  parenthood as well.

- **Race** Although race should not play a part in any hiring decision, it
  is safest to leave it off the resume completely. Membership in certain
  fraternities, sororities, or clubs might reveal ethnic background to a
  hiring manager.

- **Age** As you write a list of the community organizations in which
  you are involved, ask yourself if they reveal your age range to an
  employer. Do not reveal more than the employer needs to know!

- **Professional Affiliations** List professional associations to which
  you currently belong or have once belonged, especially if your profession values this type of affiliation. They can be listed either alpha-
  betically or in order of relevance to your profession. Note any offices
  you have held or currently hold.

- **Military**   Many resume writers with armed services experience choose to create a section that offers a brief account of their military background. If adding a military section to an otherwise civilian resume, keep the information brief and direct. Include only the branch of service, your highest rank, and the dates you served.

Honors, Awards, and Publications

Some resume writers have achieved a number of awards and honors throughout their professional career, which should be given a place to shine on the resume. Watch for these pitfalls:

- If you have received only one award in your professional career, do not use a separate section for it; instead, include it in the body of the resume or incorporate it into another section.

- Do not include awards if they suggest a pattern of recent burnout. For example, the resume reader sees that you received the "Salesperson of the Year" awards for 1995, 1996, and 1997, but there is no sign of any awards since then. If you are still in the same position, why did you stop earning the awards?

 List even those awards that might seem silly to you. You might snicker at your "Employee of the Month" award, but a potential employer won't.

Any articles, research papers, books, or chapters in books that you have authored or coauthored should be listed with the name of the publication and publication date. List your most current publication first, and go backward in time from there. You can also include in this section any invited presentations you have given. If your list of publications and presentations is quite long, you might add a third resume page as an addendum to the resume and allow them the space they deserve.

Other

The "Other" section is a great catchall section. It offers the writer a chance to squeeze a hodgepodge of information into a small space. Because of its ambiguous title, the "Other" section can include anything you want it to: all the little things that make you special that didn't quite fit in under any other section. Unlike all of the other sections, the things you list under "Other" can be unrelated to each other.

Use this section for such things as:

- Fluency in foreign languages
- Musical or artistic accomplishments
- Global travel
- Special knowledge or skills you have not yet mentioned

The Personal Section

The Personal section has engendered more disagreement over its existence than any other resume section. Informal polls indicate that about 50 percent of hiring managers think that a Personal section is a waste of resume space with no useful qualities. The other 50 percent find it a helpful, informative look at the resume writer's most interesting traits. I think that much of this disagreement stems from a difference in how the Personal section is defined and from varying opinions on what the Personal section should include. Because the Personal section offers so much room for interpretation, I've dedicated a little extra space to discussing the dos and don'ts and the pros and cons below.

AN HONEST LOOK AT THE PERSONAL SECTION

The Personal section can offer the resume reader a glimpse into the personality of the writer. It identifies intuitive skills through a listing of hobbies, personal accomplishments, travel, languages, likes, and dislikes. It can be anything that you design it to be. The main thing it should do, however, is offer a carefully chosen list of personal abilities and traits that will impress a hiring manager and move you closer to your job goals.

The Personal section is not, however, a revelation of your physical status (no height, weight, age, or health statistics)! Nor is it a place for your marital status (Don't say, "Married, two children") or for a bland string of hobbies, such as "Enjoy fishing, hiking, Euchre, and golf."

Positives and Negatives

Including the Personal section has a positive side and a negative side. Read the potential positives and negatives outlined below before making a decision about putting the Personal section on your resume.

The Potential Positives

- A well-written Personal section might pique the resume reader's interest. It might make your resume stand out from the others and tip the scales in favor of calling you in for an interview.

- Your personal interests can be a conversation starter in the interview. It gives the interviewer something light to bring up to ease the pressure.

- The interviewer might share your interests and feel a bond with you that he or she doesn't share with the other applicants. I've heard many a story about interviews that focused more on the golf game than the job; in every case, the applicant got the job offer.

- Because this section reveals information about you of a more personal nature, it makes the reader feel as if he or she knows more about you, which puts you a head above the competition.

- If your Personal section happens to touch upon skills that the employer feels would be useful on the job, he or she is much more likely to call you in for an interview and make you a job offer. Volunteering, bicycling, and community theater all translate into skills that can easily transfer to the workplace.

The Potential Negatives

- There is always the danger that you might touch upon interests that will turn the potential employer off. Because you can't possibly know the interests of everyone who might read your resume, it is difficult to avoid this possibility.

- Some employers regard the Personal section as "fluff," and might perceive the entire resume with a more critical eye if it contains this section.

- An employer might worry that a personal interest might be time-consuming and distract you from your dedication to the job.

Going for It

If you decide to include personal interests on your resume, follow these rules carefully.

DON'T include interests that could be controversial or offensive, such as hunting or gun collecting.

DON'T include dangerous hobbies, such as skydiving or rock climbing. This makes you an injury risk, and makes the personnel representative nervous.

DO be aware of stereotypes concerning certain hobbies. Remember, the resume reader will form an opinion of your personality based largely upon the personal interests you choose to include.

Write your interests in a way that reflects your leadership roles. Paint a picture of yourself as successful, active, and interesting.

For example, instead of saying, "enjoy reading and golf," say "Member of Friends of Library Avid Reader's Club. Annual participant in Cross-County Golf Charity Playoffs."

Other Examples:

WRONG:

INTERESTS: Tennis, theater, model airplanes

RIGHT:

INTERESTS: Tennis Club Tutor to Young Players. Community Theater Lighting and Sound Technician. Build quarter-scale radio-controlled model airplanes.

WRONG:

Enjoy running, bicycling, public speaking.

RIGHT:

INTERESTS: Participate in local 5k and 10k running events.
Member of Tri-State Bicyclist Club. Treasurer of local Toastmasters
chapter.

ANYTHING ELSE?

If there is anything else you feel compelled to include on your resume that
won't fit into the sections mentioned so far, feel free to make up your own
section.

You might include a section called "Military" to cover your armed services experience. You might also include sections called "Research,"
"Licenses," "Certifications," or "Lectures." Or, you might choose to
combine two related headings to save space, such as "Licenses
and Certifications." See the resumes on pages 111, 112, 113, 131, and 132
for other creative sections.

CHAPTER SUMMARY

In this chapter, you learned to use creative sections to round out your
resume with a presentation that is both logical to read and appealing to the
resume reader.

CHAPTER 12

Editing Your Resume

In this chapter, you will use the Resume Writer's Checklist to review your work against the list of resume strategies, to ensure that you have put together an outstanding resume.

At this stage, you should have written the first draft of your resume, from heading to ending. So far, your work is probably rough-edged and uneven. You might have labored hard over this rough draft, and the work might have been tedious at points, but your finished product will be well worth the effort.

The toughest part—the recollection, formulation, and sorting of information—is finally complete. You've now graduated to the easier part: the reading, analyzing, and editing of what you've done so far. This is the fun stuff! Now is your chance to reformulate and rephrase your work to give it just the flavor you want. To ensure that you've made your resume the best that it can be, review your work according to the four golden rules.

THE GOLDEN RULES OF REVIEW

Separate Yourself

Before you go about the task of reviewing and editing your resume, you must give yourself a period of separation from your work. If you have been working with it for several hours, you become numb to the nuances and phrasing, and many things that you've written stop registering clearly in your brain. It becomes impossible to analyze carefully. Allowing yourself a breather gives you a new perspective on what you've written, enabling you to see it through the prospective employer's eyes.

Share It

Don't try to edit the resume yourself. Take it to someone who knows you well and understands the work that you've done. This can be a spouse, friend, or trusted colleague. Make sure they give you honest feedback and don't withhold criticism to spare feelings. Friends are good at coming up with important accomplishments or aspects of your past positions that you might have missed. Be sure to ask them if there is anything you left out.

Study It

Now take a fresh look at what you've chosen to write. Is it saying what you had intended to say? Does it have the tone and flavor that you want to project? Mark any spots that need adjustment.

Swift and Sure Editing

Get that red pen working fast and furiously over the page to get rid of any extraneous details or poorly worded phrases. If you aren't quite giving the right slant to your skills and talents, go ahead and fiddle with them until you get them right. Don't hold back. Nobody gets it right the first time. It takes rewrite after rewrite to reach perfection.

THE RESUME WRITER'S CHECKLIST

After you feel that you have shaped your resume into the most precise, interesting, and well-presented document that it can be, give it the checklist review. This will give you the assurance that you've done everything in the best order and achieved a resume of the highest quality.

Format:

☐ Have I kept my resume to no more than two pages?

☐ Are the sections and headings consistently placed?

☐ Is it inviting to read, with plenty of white space and short bullet points?

☐ It is free from misspellings, grammatical errors, and other mistakes?

Heading:

☐ Are my name and address complete and accurate?

☐ Can I be reached easily by a potential employer?

Summary:

☐ Does my summary support my job goals?

☐ Did I write a clear job title that will identify but not pigeonhole me?

☐ Did I state accomplishments or direct learned skills in my summary?

☐ Is my summary an accurate, balanced picture of what I have to offer?

☐ Does my summary seem focused and goal-oriented?

Job Experience:

☐ Do I go back 10–15 years with my job history?

☐ Have I stressed accomplishments rather than tasks in my job description?

☐ Have I prioritized my accomplishments so that the most impressive come first?

☐ Have I avoided long, monotonous paragraphs?

☐ Have I avoided the phrase, "Responsible for"?

☐ Have I taken out all unnecessary "the's" and "and's"?

☐ Have I used plenty of action verbs?

☐ Am I emphasizing the skills that I want to use in my next job?

☐ Have I supported those skills and experiences that I highlighted in the summary?

☐ Have I avoided acronyms, esoteric terms, and vague descriptions?

☐ Have I been thorough with my job skills and accomplishments?

Education:

☐ Did I start with the highest degree earned?

☐ Did I leave off extraneous information on irrelevant courses?

☐ Did I include coursework that I took without achieving a degree?

☐ Did I indicate honors and awards received?

☐ Did I leave off school activities (unless I am a recent graduate)?

Other Sections:

☐ Did I create logical, inclusive sections for my other information?

☐ If I wrote a "personal" section, did I show off my skills, and not just interests alone?

Image:

☐ Did I create the overall professional image I had intended?

☐ Was I accurate and honest in the way I portrayed myself?

CHAPTER SUMMARY

In this chapter, you have reviewed your resume against a checklist to help you fine-tune your first draft.

CHAPTER 13

Resumes for Entry-Level Workers

In this chapter, you learn the art of writing a resume that highlights the skills of a recent graduate or entry-level worker with little prior work experience.

If you are a beginning job seeker, writing a resume will be a little tougher than if you are an experienced job hunter. Without extensive job experience to describe on the resume, you need to pay closer attention to other areas of your background to put a little meat on your resume's bones.

THE FORMAT

Without a long work history to chronicle, you probably want to concentrate on keeping your resume to the one-page format. One page should be plenty to cover your history thoroughly, and it keeps the page looking full, not flimsy.

Some experts suggest that a functional resume works best for an entry-level employee because it de-emphasizes your lack of extensive work experience. The trouble is that most people in human resources realize that this is what a functional resume is meant to do; therefore, in fact, it might actually call attention to your lack of experience. I think a chronological resume format works quite well for an entry-level worker, as long as you are clever enough to fill it with accomplishments that prove your strong skills set.

Your Summary

As an entry-level job seeker, it is especially important to identify your career goals clearly in the summary at the top of the resume. You don't have the luxury of letting your past job experience dictate your future direction. If you are unsure of your job goals, work on Chapter 3, "Setting Career Goals," again to help you recognize what is important to you and where you'd like to take your career. Employers look for and are impressed by clearly defined goals in entry-level workers.

In your summary, choose a title that relates to what your strengths and schooling support. If you graduated in graphic arts, for example, call yourself a Graphic Artist, because that is the position you hope to be hired for.

Next, highlight particular areas of interest or classes taken that support your background in the graphic arts field. You'll be following the same general template for all chronological resumes. For example:

SUMMARY: Energetic and creative Graphic Artist with particular interests in illustration and visual design. Known for distinctive ideas, persuasive skills, and ability to meet tight deadlines. Strong knowledge of:

- Quark, Illustrator, Photocopy
- Video Presentations
- PageMaker, Corel Draw
- Logo Design
- Pamphlets, Publications
- 3-D Displays

Notice that this summary leaves out the number of years of work experience. If you have less than three years of work experience, it is best not to highlight this fact.

The Education Section

Employers will be particularly interested in your educational background. They will be searching your resume's Education section for clues about your personality, work ethic, and extracurricular involvement.

Place your Education section just below the summary, where it will be easy to find and get plenty of attention. Allow your Education section to delve into more detail than it might if you had several jobs to describe. For example, you might emphasize some particular courses that you did well in, which closely relate to your career goals. Or, you might describe a student teaching experience or a course earning credits for assisting a professor with grading papers.

 Be careful when selecting courses to highlight. Steer clear of irrelevant courses and stick to those that will interest a hiring manager.

The Experience Section

Although you might feel that your time in the fast-food business was menial and not of interest to a corporate hiring manager, this is far from the truth. Hiring managers know that if you've just graduated from school, your work experience will not be very substantial. But they do want to see that you can hold a job, that you are responsible, and that you've gotten your feet wet following directions and showing up for work on schedule.

Include successful summer or after-school jobs that you have held throughout your schooling. If you were promoted within those positions, be sure to highlight that fact. If you were taught to balance out the register, keep track of the books, write the employee schedule, and so on, include these aspects of the job.

If you held an internship that relates to your field of study, write it just as you would any full-time salaried position including details of your job duties and the accomplishments you achieved during your time on the job.

Other Sections

You might want to include a "Military" section if you participated in the Reserve Officers' Training Corps (ROTC) or have other military background.

You might also want to include a section, such as "Foreign Studies" or "Studies Abroad," if you spent time overseas.

Include a section called "Honors and Awards" or "Academic Activities" to list outstanding scholastic achievements or academic fraternities/sororities. You should also list your academic activities here, such as being a member of the marketing club or an editor of the school newspaper.

Include a section called "Activities" or "Extracurricular" if you were on the football team or were a member of the drama group, a choral group, and so on. Don't list too many outside activities, though: Consider them from a potential employer's perspective and choose carefully.

DOS AND DON'TS FOR BEGINNER RESUMES

DO list any honors, awards, or high class standing on your resume.

DON'T go into great detail about wage-earning jobs you held during school or summer that don't relate to your major (waitressing, fast-food work, and so on), unless your work emphasizes leadership skills or taught you general business concepts, such as bookkeeping or customer service.

DO write your Summary in the same fashion that you would if you were an experienced employee, highlighting areas of strength.

DO list extracurricular activities, especially those related to academics or job skills.

DON'T forget to check for spelling and grammar errors. More errors are found on entry-level resumes than any other type of resume!

DO use quality bond paper and a laser-quality printer to give your resume a professional appearance.

SAMPLE RESUMES

Study the following sample resumes as you begin to write your own.

SANDY ARULF
394 Quest Drive
Colleysville, Maryland 21030
(410) 555-1987
arulf@sprynet.com

CAREER PROFILE

Marketing communicator with Fortune 500 experience. Known by management, clients, and co-workers for outstanding editing skills, initiative, ability to explain technical topics, strong work ethic, and commitment to quality. Focus on Web site development and editing. Expertise in:

- Developing communications strategies
- Working under tight deadlines
- Writing and editing Web site content
- HTML
- Teamwork
- Managing multiple projects simultaneously

PROFESSIONAL EXPERIENCE

AMERICAN LIFE INSURANCE, Seattle, WA (1998-2000)

Staff Writer

Involved in diverse facets of advertising, writing, designing, and editing brochures, publications, Web communications, and multi-media advertising.

Key Accomplishments:
- Wrote more than 40 pages of content for American Life's first product-specific Web site.
- Designed and wrote marketing brochures promoting American Life products.
- Worked with advertising account executive to develop promotional item in support of American Life-funded charitable group.
- Designed, edited, and wrote column for *NewsTopix*, a weekly newsletter for agents who sell American Life Insurance. Column received excellent reviews within first 6 months of publication.
- Assisted in writing and producing video introducing employee benefits program.

TECHNICAL SKILLS

HTML, NetObjects Fusion 2.0.1, Microsoft Word, Microsoft Excel, Microsoft Project,
Microsoft Access, DOS

EDUCATION

St. Mary's College, Seattle, WA Bachelor of Arts in Writing/Media, concentration in advertising
and public relations, 1998

CONTINUING EDUCATION

HTML class (American Life campus), 1999
American Life Emerging Leaders course, 1999

Notice that this person has only two years of professional experience, yet it seems like more. College background is downplayed, because the work experience is impressive on its own. A little more space is added between sections to fill out the page, which gives the reader the impression that this resume represents a fully experienced professional.

LESLEY WHISNER
2907 COPPERHEAD COURT
SOUTHERN CITY, SOUTH CAROLINA 19808
(307) 555-3209 RESIDENCE
(307) 555-9807 PAGER

SUMMARY

Well-organized, enthusiastic finance professional with mortgage and loan experience. Known for excellent communication skills, perseverance, and ability to work with diverse populations. Always maintain a cheerful, helpful attitude when dealing with customers and colleagues. Particular strengths include:

- Mortgage File Preparation
- Liaison with Mortgage Branches
- Investor Relations
- Recording Checks
- Spreadsheets
- Credit Reports

EDUCATION

BS, Business Administration and Finance (a five year accelerated course) 1998
John Carrol University, Raleigh, North Carolina

PROFESSIONAL EXPERIENCE

FIRST FEDERAL NATIONAL BANK, COLUMBIA, SC (Summers 1997-1998)

Quality Control Assistant

Assisted with the mortgage preparation process. Requested credit reports, appraisals, and reverifications of employment, deposits, mortgages, rent, tax returns, and loan applications. Located and prepared mortgage files for monthly audit and outside contractors and investors.

- Consistently entrusted with a large variety of mortgage-related tasks to manage and resolve independently.

- Communicated with investors regarding documentation and special requests. Received high marks on performance reviews for ability to communicate effectively.

- Recorded mortgage funding checks and wires with high rate of accuracy.

COMPANY-SPONSORED TRAINING

Lotus 1-2-3
FoxPro
MS Word
Business Communication Skills

OTHER

- Received local Citizen Award for Habitat for Humanity Project. Co-chaired community-wide charity event involving 116 people.
- Chosen to sing in chorus of local dinner theater production of "Hometown Boy"

Notice how the entry-level person with no experience other than summer jobs while attending college has managed to give herself a professional title in the Summary that points toward her goals. She places her Education section above the Professional Experience section because her experience, although it relates to her future interests, was only part-time.

GARRICK SEANING
2502 Camisky Court
Cooperstown, NY 30079
(709) 555-9060

SUMMARY: Results-driven Management Trainee with Bachelor's Degree in Business Administration with strong concentration in Information Systems. Known for writing skills, leadership ability, and team tasking. Background in:

- Business Management
- Budget Coordination
- Media Communications
- Inventory Control
- Scheduling
- Leading Meetings

TECHNICAL: BASIC I and II, FORTRAN I and II, PASCAL, COBOL I and II, C, Assembly Language, some knowledge of UNIX.

EDUCATION: Delaware State University, Canton, DE 1999
Concentration: Management
Minor: Information Systems

WORK HISTORY: **Business Manager**, Alpha Delta Phi, Delaware State University, 1998-1999

Managed daily operations of 40 member local chapter of national fraternity. Motivated members to achieve vision of campus-wide recognition and involvement.

- Created and wrote bi-weekly column for campus newspaper, and appeared as guest speaker on college station WDSU.
- Organized and coordinated fund-raising events involving up to 200 volunteers and months of preparation.
- Prepared monthly financial statements, and assessed members for dues and fees which brought books in balance.
- Inventoried household and kitchen supplies and devised improved stocking and review schedule.
- Led weekly fraternity meetings which ensured strong communication among members. Created, scheduled, and led quarterly "Think Tank" sessions, which included school faculty members.

OTHER: Member of Student-Faculty Planning Commission, 1998
Assistant Director, Drama Club Production of *House Guest*

Notice how this resume makes great use of unpaid college experience to fill out the Work History section. Garrick used the title "Management Trainee" as the position he hopes to obtain, which will incorporate his business and information systems backgrounds.

LORRAINE SCHURENBERG
9507 Booker Drive Swampscott, MA 34870 (409) 555-9089 LSCHUR@HOME.com

SUMMARY

Organized and results-oriented Computer Programming Professional with background in Education. Known for communication skills, ability to prioritize, and effective planning. Strengths include:

- FORTRAN
- COBOL
- Pascal
- C
- Basic
- Unix

TECHNICAL SKILLS

Programming: PDP-11 (Basic language); VAX/VMS (FORTRAN ans pascal languages)

Software: Lotus 1-2-3, Microsoft Excel, Microsoft Word, WordPerfect, and Microsoft Access.

EXPERIENCE

Bryant Woods Elementary, Columbia, MA   1997-Present
Teacher, Grades 3 and 4

Developed lesson plans to capture imagination of students and engage them in the learning process. Commanded classroom respect in a positive learning atmosphere.

- Developed and wrote class curriculum, much of which was adopted by fellow faculty.
- Created, wrote, and implemented structured lesson plans, which were able to be individualized according to student ability.
- Evaluated student skills, and placed in groups according to level. Consistently assessed student progress to ensure correct group placement.

EDUCATION

B.S., COMPUTER AND INFORMATION SCIENCES, Swampscott Community College
    Cum Laude
    Courses in BASIC I and II, FORTRAN I and II, Pascal, COBOL I and II, C,
Assembly
    Language, and Software Engineering.

B.S. ELEMENTARY EDUCATION, Xavier University, Clermont, MA

PROFESSIONAL TRAINING in communication skills, planning, and organization.

In this resume, Lorraine's schooling in computer systems is emphasized, because her professional experience is in a completely unrelated field. Her teaching experience is visible but downplayed, and her technical skills and computer degree are designed to dominate the resume's presentation.

CHAPTER SUMMARY

In this chapter, you have learned the keys to writing an entry-level resume that emphasizes the qualities that are of interest to hiring managers.

CHAPTER 14

Resumes for Career Changers

In this chapter, you learn to write a resume that highlights the skills that employers look for when you change careers.

TODAY'S WORK WORLD

Changing careers is becoming a commonplace occurrence in the world of work today. Because of unstable work environments, people find themselves without a job or decide to move on to new positions as many as 10 times or more during their career.

Why Do People Change Careers?

People change careers for a variety of reasons. Sometimes it is because they have moved to a new location and can no longer find work in their field. Other times the field changes, and they find that their skills have become obsolete. Still others have reached a point in their careers at which they can no longer find satisfaction with their work or their needs and interests have changed.

FIRST THINGS FIRST

The first thing you must do when deciding to change careers is to carefully identify your new needs and career goals. Do not attempt to write a resume until you have explored your new direction. Examine your needs and goals with respect to the following topics.

First, make sure you really do want to change career paths. If you question your decision, you will never be able to take the necessary steps to see it through. Explore your reasons for wanting to change careers. Is it because you are burned out with the company, the people, and the job duties? Is it because you need to make more money? Or, is it because you want to work in a different job environment? Before changing careers, make sure your reasons are justified, and that your dissatisfaction couldn't be cured by simply making small changes within the same career (like changing companies or going for a promotion).

Next, examine your skills, abilities, education, and experience in relation to your new career choice. Do you have the skills and training necessary to move into your chosen career field?

Finally, explore the direction you'd like your new career to take. Is there room for advancement and growth? Will this change be a good long-term investment for you?

YOUR RESUME

If you have finalized your decision to change careers, and you are sure of your new direction, it is time to begin writing your resume. Your new resume must market those skills and accomplishments that will transfer well into your chosen field. These are the skills that your future employer will recognize as being valuable to the job that he or she has in mind for you.

These skills might come from the workplace, have been learned independently, or might have been learned through formal education.

 Career changers must identify and emphasize transferable skills on their new resume.

Chronological Versus Functional Format

Some resume experts suggest the functional resume format for career changers, because this format emphasizes skill sets over job experience. If you decide to use a functional format, be sure to keep plenty of information about your work experience on the resume so that it doesn't look like you are hiding anything. Keep dates, job titles, and brief job descriptions separate for each position.

Otherwise, the chronological format works well for career changers, as long as the skills and accomplishments you emphasize are those that potential employers in your new field will find interesting. This simply involves careful writing on your part, to downplay skills that will no longer be needed and to emphasize those that your new employer will find impressive.

DOS AND DON'TS FOR CAREER CHANGERS

DO state your intended new career title specifically in your summary on your new resume.

DON'T sound wishy-washy about your strengths or transferable skills.

DO include a cover letter with your new resume that explains your interest in your new career field.

DON'T decide to change careers based on the money factor alone: Choose a career that you think you will enjoy (despite the salary influence), and the money will follow. Otherwise, you might end up changing again sooner than you think.

DO work to make connections in your new field. A new resume will help, but personal connections in the field will open doors for you a lot faster.

DO emphasize transferable intuitive skills as well as learned skills on your new resume.

Study the following sample resumes that career changers wrote to enter their new field. Note how they emphasized the skills from their previous jobs that would transfer well into their new positions. They also highlighted personal skills that would be useful in their new career.

Emilie Ericson
1 Judith Place
Montclair, NE 60750
(404) 555-7698

OBJECTIVE: **EVENTS COORDINATOR**

SUMMARY: Energetic and creative administrative professional with over 6 years experience in corporate marketing setting. Known for public relations skills, diplomacy with customers, and cooperative, resourceful attitude. Special skills include:

- Heavy Client Contact
- Organizing Conferences and Meetings
- Scheduling
- Slide and Video preparation
- Business Communications
- Interdepartmental Liaison

EXPERIENCE: **BALLEN AND KLINGMAN, INC MOORE , NE 1995-1999**
Administrative Assistant

Assisted Director of Marketing with organizational duties and business communications. Oversaw meeting planning and extensive travel arrangements. Created documents using Word and Powerpoint.

- Organized heavy travel schedule of more than 12 days per month at any of 17 satellite sites.
- Arranged the scheduling, supplies, and interoffice communications for bi-weekly staff meetings.
- Coordinated site location of annual conference for 200+ employees, and acted as liaison between corporate headquarters and site planners.
- Dealt courteously with clients and customers to ensure service satisfaction.

TRENTON PHILLIPS, INC HEBRON, NE 1992-1995
Clerical Assistant

Acted as receptionist and administrative assistant in busy marketing division of clothing retailer.

- Assisted in the creative development of presentation pieces including slides and video for national conference attended by more than 1,000 staff and clients.
- Coordinated telephone calls through 20-line system to management and staff of two departments.
- Acted a liaison for Marketing and Sales Management offices. Worked diligently to ensure consistent flow of communication.

EDUCATION: Diploma, Maryvale High School, Maryvale NE

CONTINUING
EDUCATION:

Business Correspondence	1996
Microsoft Word	1997
Powerpoint	1998

Emilie's resume does all it can to emphasize the skills that she believes will transfer from her administrative background into her new field of event planning. Although much of her former job experience has involved typing, sorting mail, and other such administrative tasks, she gave these duties very little mention. She instead focuses strongly on those skills that she might use as an event coordinator, such as scheduling, working with clients, and arranging meetings.

DEBRA OSTROWSKI
1524 Norwood Place
Towson, CA 21098
(410)-555-9086
debo@HOME.com

OBJECTIVE: Travel Agent

SUMMARY

Dedicated and outgoing travel industry professional with more than 4 years experience assisting clients with travel needs. Known for creative solutions, efficient work habits, and friendly, positive rapport with customers. Thorough knowledge of CRS, Computerized Reservations System. Particular expertise includes:
- Rate Schedules
- Auto Rental Policies
- Computer Reservations
- Airline Reservation Systems
- National Routing Services
- Map Reading

EXPERIENCE

DAVIS CAR RENTALS, Los Angeles, CA 1995-1999
Reservationist

Spoke with customers and assessed needs. Explained rates and policies, and scheduled reservations via CRS, computerized Reservation system. Examined data from National Highway Administration and discerned most appropriate route for customers.

- Elected Employee of the Month Award 3 consecutive months, based on friendly and reliable service to customers.
- Highest Rental Reservation Rate for 1997 and 1998, with over 1,500 rentals concluded with top level satisfaction rating.
- Knowledgeable regarding travel information throughout U.S., Canada, and Mexico.
- Familiar with Customs Inspection requirements and passport needs.

U-HAUL-IT, Los Angeles, CA 1993-1995
Front Desk Receptionist

Reserved vans and trucks for customers with local and national hauling needs. Explained rates and rental policies. Completed and reviewed forms using computerized tracking system.

- Revised Vehicle Tracking Form to increase accuracy of scheduling system which reduced rate of vehicle down time.
- Managed heavy volume of transactions with low error rate and high rate of customer satisfaction.

EDUCATION

Villa Julie College, Towson, CA Secretarial Science Certificate December 1992

This job seeker wants to change careers from clerical worker to travel agent. She makes this clear in her objective. The skills and job functions that she emphasizes point toward her ability to excel in the travel industry.

CHAPTER SUMMARY

In this chapter, you examined your career needs and goals, and then applied this to create a resume that is focused on your new direction.

CHAPTER 15

Resumes for Information Technology (IT) or Technical Workers

In this chapter, you learn what hiring managers are looking for in resumes for high-tech positions and how to create a resume that highlights your technical skills without disregarding your intuitive skills.

FLUFF-FREE ZONE

In my experience as a career counselor and resume writer, I have found that you technical folks—from computer programmers to engineers—can be a cautious and downright obstinate bunch. Technical job seekers tend to have a strong orientation toward facts, figures, and logical thinking, and not much enthusiasm for a salesy, marketing-type resume approach. "The hiring managers want to see my technical skills without a lot of fluff," you tell me, in response to my suggestions that you put a little personality into your resume.

Well, you are right about the fluff part. Hiring managers are much too busy to waste time wading through fluff. But fluff isn't what the technical resume needs. What it *does* need is a bit of personality to turn it from a dry, monotonous list of technical skills into a lively account of what you can do *and how well you can do it.*

THE RESUME THAT STANDS OUT

Put yourself in the hiring manager's place. Pretend you have one opening for a person to convert a system from a UNISYS environment to an IBM environment. If you have 60 resumes in a pile on your desk that all say that they can do systems conversion, how will you know which of the 60 people to hire? Because most technical resumes simply include a rote list of skills, they tend to look alike; therefore, it's hard to tell whom to hire.

The resume that stands out from the crowd tells the hiring manager not only that the applicant can do systems conversion, but also that he or she can do it *well.* How do you get your resume to do this? Think about what it is that makes you good at your job! Consider what it is that makes you better than the guy at the next desk.

If you have a tough time thinking of something off the top of your head, think about your boss. Is he or she happy with your work? Why? Besides your technical skills, what does your boss base his or her assessment of your work on? Do you get performance reviews, and if so, what criteria do they base your performance upon? These, then, are the skills and qualities that hiring managers for positions like yours care about!

Consider these examples of technical work traits that hiring managers love to see and apply them to your own situation if possible:

- **Work completed on time or ahead of schedule**   This saves the company money.
- **Attention to detail**   This tells them that your error rate is low, your failure rate is minimal, and your work is of the highest quality.
- **Ability to motivate team members and coworkers**   This tells them that when you are associated with an assignment, it runs smoothly and gets done well.

- **Ability to guide junior workers through a task**   This tells them that you can teach others by careful training and good example.

- **Ability to work independently**   This tells them that you aren't constantly running to the boss for direction or support.

- **A good attitude**   This tells them that you are flexible with project changes and aren't grumbling over company decisions.

- **A willingness to learn**   This tells them that you aren't balking at new technologies or changes in the old system.

- **Perseverance**   This tells them that you are able to see a long-term assignment through from conception to completion.

- **Creative thinking**   This tells them that you are able to see your way around a roadblock and reconfigure your strategy when necessary.

- **Devotion to the company**   This tells them that they can feel confident that you won't take the technical expertise you've learned from them and hawk it to another high-tech firm, leaving them high and dry in the middle of a project.

ACCOMPLISHMENTS

Many technical types tell me that they simply do their assignments as requested, and no great accomplishments are possible in their job. Yet, if we sit down and think long enough, we are always able to pull up a nice, impressive list of accomplishments beyond the daily work requirements.

Use these same traits listed above to write a list of specific accomplishments that you have achieved beyond your daily duties. Consider each of the positions you have held and the individual projects you have worked on. Always answer the question: *How did you do the job well?*

Study the following sample technical resumes. Note how they include a complete listing of technical skills and knowledge while infusing the resume with personality at the same time.

TAYLOR WILLOWS
5775 McCarron Ct.
West Chester, OH 45069
(513) 555-1251
E-mail: Twillows@AOL.com

PROFILE

Senior level Programmer/Analyst with over 8 years experience in analyzing and solving complex programming problems. Write, test, troubleshoot, and maintain programs for diverse applications. Known for excellent communication skills, perseverance, and attention to quality. Technical expertise includes:

    *Database Development   *System Implementation
    *Programming Specifications   *Cost-Benefit Analysis
    *Structured Analysis and Design   *System Documentation

TECHNICAL SKILLS

    Hardware: IBM 3033, 4341

    Software: VSAM, CICS, ANS COBOL, TSO/ISPF, DOS/JCL, OS/JCL

EXPERIENCE

FIRST FEDERAL BANK AND TRUST   Glendale, CA   1998-Present
Senior Systems Analyst

Analyze, design, and implement systems for equities department and the division of personnel. Conduct cost-benefit analysis and feasibility studies for new equipment proposals. Oversee hardware maintenance and perform program troubleshooting.

- Designed and implemented complex Personnel Tracking System (PTS) in COBOL/VSAM environment.
- Met with user groups to discuss and design enhancements to system. Commended for quick response time and ability to coordinate diverse needs into coherent system.
- Received Superior Efficiency Award for development of efficient systems operation that responds quickly to user needs.
- Designed and implemented the Remote Client Access System to support customer on-line access, via PC, to their personal account information.

COLUMBIA BANK AND TRUST   Laurel, MD   1992-1998
Programmer/Analyst

Designed and analyzed Mortgage Loan and Installment Loan Application programs. Emphasis on language efficiency and easy maintenance. Defined and resolved program malfunctions.

- Chosen as Project Lead Assistant on Mortgage Loan and Installment Loan projects.
- Designed, coded, and tested Mortgage Trial Balance System and Installment Loan Update.

EDUCATION

    FISK UNIVERSITY, Nashville, TN   B.S. Computer Sciences   1992

Notice that Taylor placed her technical skills toward the top of the resume because of their importance to her field. She also emphasized accomplishments she had achieved beyond her typical duties.

JOHN BERTO
9807 Tremont Road
Lexington, KY 40985
(609) 555-3496

PROFILE: Energetic and results-oriented Information Technology professional with mainframe and AS400 experience in Fortune 200 manufacturing environment. Consistently recognized for problem solving and follow through. Strengths include the following:

- Systems Design
- Software Development
- Accounting
- Customer Service and Sales

- Database Management
- User Interface
- Troubleshooting
- Teamwork

PROFESSIONAL EXPERIENCE: WICKINS MICROBIOLOGY SYSTEMS, Berea, KY (1984-1996)

Senior Programmer Analyst/Project Leader (1987-1996)
Developed and supported application software for Order Processing, Accounts Receivable, Finance, Sales, Accounts Payable, Payroll and General Ledger within several different divisions.

- Supported Software 2000 Accounts Payable and General Ledger systems using RPG400, Query and COBOL.
- Developed Accounts Receivable system using RPG400 and subfiles for three separate divisions originating credit hold functions and shortening monthly closing.
- Designed in-house Payroll Labor Distribution system using RPG400 and subfiles that interfaced with Software 2000 General Ledger system and eliminated manual transaction updates.
- Participated in conversion of European Order Processing system to meet needs of all divisions and interfacing with multiple manufacturing systems. Ensured conversion and accuracy of orders from IMS/DL1 Mainframe databases to AS400.
- Maintained application software using COBOL and CICS for on-line and batch programming on the IBM4381 within Order Processing, Accounts Receivable, Finance, Sales, Bill of Materials, Material Control, Accounts Payable, General Ledger, and Payroll during conversion to the AS400.

Database Administrator   (1984-1987)
Developed and maintained IMS/DL1 Databases. Supported the Systems and Programming staff in development of new systems and maintenance of existing systems.

- Developed IMS/DL1 Databases for Quality Control, Lot Inventory Control, Lot Staging, and Procurement System.
- Developed programs using COBOL, CICS, and IMS/DL1 for all databases, both interactive and batch.

EDUCATION: Sussex Community College, Sussex, Kentucky AA, Computer Sciences, 1983

TECHNICAL SKILLS:

Hardware	- IBM 370, IBM 4381, System 38, AS400
Software	- OS/MVS, VSAM, MVS OS/JCL, CICS, IBM Utilities, IMS/DL-1, COBOL, RPG III or RPG400, Query, SQL
PC Packages	- Windows, WordPerfect, Excel, Access, Microsoft Project, Word

COURSES: Ongoing professional development in PC, mid-range, and mainframe systems/applications.

This resume incorporates longer accomplishments bullets into the body of the text, and because there is space for them, they work well. He kept the resume concise by reducing his extensive list of ongoing professional development courses to a single statement.

GIGI SHELTRAW
56 Onward Road
Emilyville, MD 21224
(410) 555-9456

PROFILE

Team-focused and results-oriented research scientist with solid track record in microbial and molecular diagnostics and solutions for biomedical and clinical companies. Achievements gained through laboratory testing, research and development of Strand Displacement Amplification (SDA), DNA probe technology and troubleshooting. Strengths include the following:

- Clinical sample processing/BSL-3 trained
- SDA technologies
- Experimental design
- NCCLS, FDA guidelines & recommendations (compliance & regulations)

- Technical writing & documentation
- Clinical diagnostic instrumentation/Elisa testing
- PC applications (MS Word, Excel, WP)
- Packaging and shipping infectious substances (certification)

PROFESSIONAL EXPERIENCE

FARBER DIAGNOSTICS, Braintree, MA   (1992 - Present)

Medical Technologist
Perform preliminary and confirmatory tests on clinical specimen.

- Perform analysis of cultured clinical specimen and identification and susceptibility of pathogenic microorganisms.
- Ensure quality control of media and reagents.
- Recognize problems, document remedial action for QC failures.
- Provide clients with result interpretation, resolve problems, and accurately record, monitor, and report test results in timely manner.
- Utilize computer software to check test status, results entry, and generation of worksheet reports.
- Maintain instrumentation, calibration, and quality control.

SIMARON KLINE MICROBIOLOGY SYSTEMS, Lynn MA   (1986 - 1992)

Associate Scientist
Team member of sample processing and generation of data from specimen with mycobacteria on diagnostic instrument.

- Designed and conducted experiments utilizing SDA/tSDA technologies. Data used in algorithm evaluation.
- Coordinated preparation and maintenance of proficiency and precision panels for clinical trials.
- Developed limit of detection and interference studies protocol for regulatory studies.
- Developed internal amplification control chemistries.
- Designed and executed quality control experiments for functional QC of raw materials, finished reagents and working test devices and kit stability studies.
- Demonstrated feasibility for direct detection of TB/genus.

EDUCATION

M.S., Microbiology, FELLERTON UNIVERSITY, Omaha, NE 1992 GPA: 3.6/4.0
Awards: *Charles Parker Award*
Graduate Teaching Assistantship.
   Beta Kappa Chi Scientific Honor Society

B.S., Biological Sciences, SYCAMORE COLLEGE, ICATHA, NY   1986
Awards: *Valco Award, CMB Scholarship*

ASSOCIATIONS

American Society for Microbiology (ASM)
American Chemist's Society (ACS)

PUBLICATIONS

Sheltraw, T Mink, & B.G. Dresino. Biodegradation of Pathogenic Microorganisms by Pseudomonas.
Journal of the American Chemists' Society. Vol. 97, Pg. 2056, 1083.

Co-author of four scientific publications (in review).

Notice the listing of awards and scholarships in the Education section even though the college degrees were earned quite a few years ago. Gigi also made sure to mention her membership in scientific professional organizations, because these are important in her line of work.

CHAPTER SUMMARY

In this chapter, you learned to write a technical resume that highlights not only your technical expertise, but also your unique qualities that make you stand out from the crowd.

CHAPTER 16

Resumes for Administrative Workers

In this chapter, you learn to create a resume that supports your goal of an administrative position by highlighting the key skills and qualities that hiring managers look for.

SHOWCASING THE RIGHT SKILLS

Some of the toughest resume challenges come from attempting to create a document that seems alive and interesting from a set of tedious technical skills. Administrative resume writers face just such a challenge, because many of their skill sets are technical in nature and must appear with emphasis throughout the resume. Things like typing, word processing, filing, writing business letters, and answering telephones are all important skills that must be highlighted, but must not be allowed to overpower the resume's tone.

Don't Forget Intuitive Skills

As an administrative person, you realize how important it is for your positive attitude and good work ethic to permeate your job environment. Although you might be working at a word processor for much of your day, it is imperative that you have a good working relationship with your managers and coworkers and that you understand their needs. Potential employers understand this too.

Employers find administrative resumes very frustrating to read, because most offer too few clues as to the personality of the writer. They can see that you are a fast typist, but what they want to know is whether you can establish good working relationships that are so important to a healthy, productive work environment.

Key Intuitive Skills Hiring Managers Look For

When hiring administrative personnel of all levels, hiring managers are particularly tuned in to these key personality traits:

- **Positive Attitude**   A cheerful, friendly demeanor is a highly prized commodity in administrative personnel. It tells the potential employer that you will treat clients courteously; you will be a pleasant, positive force around the office; and that you will handle stressful situations without undue complaints.

- **Willingness to Learn**   A productive administrative person must be flexible enough to try new things and to change old habits without a fight. Clerical workers must be open to new technology and willing to learn new systems.

- **Conscientious**   Employers hope to hire administrative workers who care about the results of their work. They want someone who is productive around the office and sees to it that assignments are completed accurately and in a timely manner.

- **Independent**   Employers need to know they can count on work being completed even without your being monitored. This gives them great peace of mind and frees them up to tackle other things. Of course, they also need to know that if you run into problems, you will seek help when necessary.

- **Reliable**   An employer counts on his or her administrative team to be there when they are needed. If an administrative worker has a habit of spotty attendance or tends to show up late on a regular basis, productivity suffers. Dependability is a strong asset in administrative circles.

WRITING PERSONALITY INTO YOUR RESUME

You know that employers will be scanning your administrative resume not only for technical skills, but for intuitive skills as well. How do you write them into the resume so that they get noticed? There are three tricks that you can use to incorporate intuitive skills into your administrative resume. Try any or all of these to create a resume that highlights personality skills:

1. **Write them into the summary**   Don't forget that much of the initial 20- to 30-second scan you will get from an employer will be concentrated on the Summary section you have written. Although it is important to emphasize your technical skills here, don't neglect to highlight that great personality!

(Intuitive skills are underlined)

Courteous and efficient Administrative Professional with six years of experience in a large corporate setting. Strong background in business writing, word processing, and direct customer communications. Known for accuracy, dependability, and high productivity, even in high-pressure situations. Special expertise in:

- Microsoft Word
- Internet research
- Letter writing

- Scheduling arrangements
- Event planning
- Graphics design

---

2. **Use other sections**   Because resumes are somewhat flexible beasts, you can be a bit creative in getting the word out that you have the intuitive skills an employer needs. Try adding a section, such as "ACTIVITIES" or "PERSONAL," to show off your personality characteristics. Just be sure to concentrate on those characteristics that the employer will find impressive. For example:

ACTIVITIES:

- Solo Expedition to Italy and Greece,   1994

- 3rd Place, Mason Area Poetry Competition,   1996

- Tutor, 4th grade math and science, evenings   1995–1998

PERSONAL: Co-coordinator, Local S.A.F.E. chapter

Library Volunteer Storytime Assistant

Social Chairman, Neighborhood Community Association

An employer will recognize reliability, a positive attitude, conscientiousness, and other skills, such as organization and communication skills.

3. **Write them into the resume**   Plugging intuitive skills into your resume throughout your job descriptions and skills presentations perks the resume up and allows it to reflect your personality. Put them anywhere and everywhere!

EXAMPLE:

BEFORE: Typed documents and letters on Microsoft Word. Sent copies to appropriate departments for review.

WITH INTUITIVE SKILLS ADDED: Created accurate and timely documents and letters on Microsoft Word. Facilitated interoffice communication by reliably forwarding copies to appropriate departments for review.

Following are some more sample resumes for you to review.

ELLEN THORNTON
6447 Westview Drive
Washington, DC 50090
(202) 555-9403
Email: EllenT @AOL.com

SUMMARY

Results oriented Administrative Secretary with over 10 years diverse experience in large corporate settings. Known for careful planning, organizational skills, diplomacy with customers, and creative thinking. Strengths include:

- Vendor Negotiations
- Written and Oral Communication Skills
- Word/Windows Expertise
- Leadership and Supervisory Ability

PROFESSIONAL EXPERIENCE

CENCOR, INC. Baltimore, MD (1994-2000)
Secretary II (1996-2000)
Secretary I (1994-1996)

Supervised two assistants in the administration of Business Services division at 5,000+ employee headquarters site. Wrote and distributed business correspondence to 16 regional offices using Word for Windows, e-mail, fax, and delivery services. Negotiated with vendors for office supplies and services for headquarters offices.

- Received several monthly bonuses since hire date for outstanding performance.
- Improved efficiency of internal communication by creating a less complex correspondence system.
- Commended for fostering a friendly and cooperative workplace atmosphere through consistent system of training and incentives for assistants.
- Promoted to supervisory position after only 2 years at company.

NATIONAL MANAGEMENT SERVICES CORPORATION, Cockeysville, MD (1990-1994)
Administrative Secretary

Assisted General Manager with business correspondence, meeting planning, and travel arrangements. Oversaw organization of supply inventory for management offices. Created documents and visuals for meetings and training sessions.

- Received company award for helpful, positive attitude.
- Developed Company Presentation Packet materials which were used to train new employees and received excellent feedback on questionnaires.
- Created a more systematic method of inventory management which resulted in fewer cost overruns and more satisfied employees.

EDUCATION

BS, Business Administration, Towson State University, Towson, MD (1989) GPA: 3.65

Ellen's resume remains upbeat from start to finish, and it emphasizes the contributions she made to both companies by being a conscientious employee.

ELISE BENNETT

399 Boxwind Lane Boston, MA 21204
(617) 555-8907 elbe@erols.com

PROFILE: Senior Office Administrator with over 18 years of progressive responsibility and diverse experience in the legal profession. Particular areas of expertise include:

- Human Resources
- Training & Development
- Recruiting/Hiring
- Budget Administration
- Workflow Management
- Space Planning

Committed self-starter who takes pride in work.

PROFESSIONAL EXPERIENCE: JUSTIR, BALDWIN AND DILLON, LLP, Boston, MA (1981-Present)

Office Administrator 1991-Present
Manage daily operation of office including personnel administration, recruiting, interviewing, hiring, training and development, workflow, personnel and payroll records, legal staff orientation, financial functions, physical facilities, office equipment, systems and procedures.

Selected Accomplishments:
- Increased the lawyer to secretary ratio from 1:1 to 2:1
- Operated office within expense budget
- Developed and implemented support staff training programs which enhanced all levels of computer and secretarial skills

Administrative Coordinator 1981-1991
(Labor & Employment Law and Real Estate Departments)
Supervised 20 secretarial support staff. Managed daily workflow assignments, reviewed and reported monthly departmental financial reports, and trained new secretaries in departmental procedures.

Selected Accomplishments:
- Installed system of practices and procedures in two departments where central supervision had not previously existed
- Created and implemented accounts receivable system which increased cash-low
- Designed and formatted financial reports which increased user-friendliness for Attorneys

OTHER EXPERIENCE: Corporate Secretary, WILSON REAL ESTATE, INC., Boston, MA (1974-1981)

EDUCATION: COLLEGE OF NOTRE DAME, Boston, MA General Education (36 credits) 1973

AFFILIATIONS: Notary Public of the State of Massachusetts 1980 to Present
Member, Association of Legal Administrators, 1991 to Present

CERTIFICATES:
- Time and Stress Management, The Notre Dame School of Continuing Studies, 1990
- Strategic Supervision, The Notre Dame School of Continuing Studies, 1990

TECHNICAL EXPERIENCE:
- Typing 80 WPM
- MicroSoft Office 97 (includes WORD97)
- Working knowledge of Excel, PowerPoint, Access, Internet

This resume does an excellent job of incorporating results into the accomplishments. Elise is even able to quantify some of her results, which adds a more powerful feel to her achievements.

REBECCA BRANDT
3165 Marilee Avenue
Cheviot, IN 31234
(617) 555-9562

PROFILE

Executive Assistant with strong professional, organizational and communications background in large legal office setting. Fluent in Spanish and English. Known for dependability, integrity, and ability to prioritize effectively. Strengths include:

- Research
- Analyzing Reports

- Communication Skills
- Document Preparation

PROFESSIONAL EXPERIENCE

BARRON AND DORRING LAW OFFICES, Caldwell, IN   (1999-Present)

Legal Assistant

Screen clients, conduct preliminary investigations and legal research; prepare and file legal documents; analyze medical records and incident reports for facts and accuracy; and collect data by communicating with medical, economic, and engineering experts.

Selected Accomplishments:

- Developed "form" documents that interfaced with data system which increased efficiency of documentation.

- Created weekly "Office Reports" that assist attorneys with scheduling of cases and facilitate interoffice communication.

- Receive consistent positive feedback from clients and colleagues regarding persistence and thoroughness when researching a case.

EDUCATION

BS, Business Administration, JERSEY CITY STATE COLLEGE, Jersey City, New Jersey 1992
Honors received: Magna Cum Laude, G.P.A. 3.7

SKILLS AND LANGUAGES

- Familiar with various office equipment (copiers, Dictaphones) and computer systems
- Proficient in DOS, MS Office: Word, Excel; Internet, WordPerfect, and Day-Timer Organizer
- Functional use of MS PowerPoint
- Proficient in Communication World (Travel Industry Software)
- Fluent in English and Spanish.

Rebecca emphasizes her bilingual skills by mentioning them twice on the resume and by choosing a section title that highlights her language abilities.

JANET McCARTHY
47 Glenacre Drive
Chartertown, OH 45908
(513) 555-5672

PROFILE

Executive Administrative Professional providing comprehensive planning, organization and administrative support to Chairmen and CEOs of global Fortune 500 companies for the past 8 years. Recognized by management for good judgment, business knowledge, collaborative relationships, discretion, and autonomy. Strengths include:

- Project Management
- Meeting Planning/Coordination
- Corporate Travel
- Trade Show and Expos

- Vendor Contracting/Relations
- Organizational Interface/Coordination
- PC Applications
  (Microsoft Office 97, Windows)

PROFESSIONAL EXPERIENCE

HERON-FEINE INTERNATIONAL, Petersburg, OH   (1996 - Present)

Executive Administrative Assistant to the Chairman & CEO
Provided administrative support including scheduling meetings, managing corporate travel, developing agendas for executive committee meetings, serving as team member on special projects.

SELECTED ACCOMPLISHMENTS:
- Negotiated and monitored performance agreements with commercial airlines, hotels and car rental vendors
- Identified and implemented cost saving procedures for travel to European divisions
- Organized on-site admin. office at trade show with selections of Modular Systems Furniture vendor
- Arranged and coordinated executive committee meetings

MOTORCOM INC, Dayton, OH   (1992 - 1996)

Administrative Assistant to Managing Director
Compiled business plans, made travel reservations, and coordinated calendar for all meetings. Organized all start-up requirements for new firm: selected office space, worked with contractor, selected and ordered furniture, coordinated with all vendors. Managed office and seven staff.

SELECTED ACCOMPLISHMENTS:

- Negotiated discount agreements for office furniture and equipment
- Supervised day to day operations
- Served as liaison with building management and construction contractors

EDUCATION/COURSES

OHIO STATE, Associates Degree, Business Administration 1992
IMMACULATA COLLEGE, Immaculata, PA, Personnel Management Courses
AMERICAN MANAGEMENT ASSOCIATION, New York, NY, Administrative Assistant Seminar

AFFILIATIONS/MEMBERSHIPS

American Business Women's Association, Middle Valley Chapter, Dayton, OH

TECHNICAL SKILLS

Computer Skills – Windows 95 – Office 97
(Microsoft Word 7.0, Excel 7.0, Power Point 7.0, Organizer '97, Palm Desktop, Calendar Creator Plus, LotusNotes 4.0)

Janet's Summary section paints her as a take-charge person who gets things done. Her strong technical skills section backs that up. She also emphasizes her negotiation skills throughout her resume.

CHAPTER SUMMARY

In this chapter, you have learned to write an administrative resume that draws attention to your intuitive skills as well as your administrative strengths.

CHAPTER 17

The New Age of Electronic Resumes

In this chapter, you learn to create a resume that is computer friendly. You'll examine what makes a resume scannable, searchable, and e-mail compatible.

WHAT ARE ELECTRONIC RESUMES?

Electronic resumes are paperless resumes in electronic form that travel by computer instead of by mail truck and are designed to do the same thing that paper resumes do: land you a job interview that leads to an offer. The way that they are different is the way that employers use them: They enjoy letting electronic databases store, sort, and conduct matches on resumes instead of doing all the initial grunt-work themselves.

While paper resumes are designed to catch the attention of the human eye, electronic resumes are designed to grab the attention of a computer. To make your resume computer-savvy, you need to understand what keywords the computer might be seeking. Depending upon the employer's needs, you might be required to prepare a resume that is:

- **Scannable:** Formatted for computerized scanning
- **Searchable:** Uses the correct keywords for database searching
- **Uploadable:** Stored in a file format that is familiar to the computer on which it will be stored

Let's examine these three considerations.

YOUR SCANNABLE RESUME

Scanning is a process by which your paper resume is transformed into electronic data, and then entered into an automated resume tracking system. The tracking system can then perform candidate searches by reviewing your resume against a set of qualifications to see if there is a potential match. The goal of the scanning system is to save hours of staff time by letting the initial and often rote weeding-out process be done by computer.

Many companies that have used scanning technology are finding that there are limitations to this system. They often lose valuable data due to conditions beyond their control, such as formatting or text quality. Some companies are moving toward newer versions of applicant tracking systems, which enter electronic resumes into a database without scanning. It is best before sending a resume to check with an employer about the type of system he or she uses, if any.

 Because resume-scanning equipment is expensive, only very large companies tend to use it.

15 Tips for a Scannable Resume

Follow these specifications to ensure that your resume can be scanned cleanly, with 100 percent recognition by the scanning hardware and software.

1. Do not send faxed copies or photocopies of your resume; they tend to scan poorly. Send originals only!

2. Stick with common sans serif fonts (nothing fancy), in a standard font size 10 to 14. Helvetica and Courier are good scanning fonts.

3. Place your name at the top of the page on its own line. Many resume scanners interpret the first line of the resume as your name, no matter what is written on that line!

4. Use standard address format below the name.

5. List each phone number on its own line. Remember, no parentheses!

6. Do not use a two-column format anywhere on the resume.

7. Use white or very light standard size ($8^{1}/_{2}$" × 11") paper, printed on one side only.

8. Use plain text with no graphics, shading, italics, underlining, or bolding.

9. Do not use tabs. Use the spacebar to indent text.

10. Do not use parentheses or brackets.

11. Avoid using horizontal or vertical lines.

12. Use wide margins around the text.

13. Use a high-quality laser printer. Dot matrix printers are difficult for the scanner to read.

14. Do not use paper clips or staples on your resume.

15. Avoid compressed lines of text.

 Do not fold your scannable resume. This makes it difficult for the scanner to handle. Use an envelope big enough to handle your unfolded resume.

After following these guidelines for a scannable resume, you will see that the scannable resume is only a distant cousin to the typical paper resume meant for the eyes of hiring managers. All of the bells and whistles meant to attract the eye's attention have been removed.

Before sending a scannable resume, it is best to inquire if one is needed. Because a scannable resume is much less reader-friendly to the human eye, it should be sent to an employer only if specifically requested.

What Happens Next?

When your resume arrives at the employer's office, it will be placed face-down in a scanner, which will translate your resume into an electronic document that might look very different from the typical paper resume. Most likely, the actual resume you sent will be thrown away once it has been scanned, never getting a single review by human eyes.

Now that your scanned resume is in the company database, it can be accessed by hiring managers throughout the organization, even from remote locations. If the computer has a tracking system, a manager can ask the computer to review resumes according to up to 60 key words per position. These might focus on job title, technical expertise, education, geographic location, or years of experience. The computer then searches its database, matches resumes, and ranks candidates according to those keywords.

YOUR SEARCHABLE RESUME

A growing number of companies request that you submit your resume to them online. You often see this option when reviewing company Web pages with job sites or when dealing with resume posting services. In this case, you upload your resume's text directly to their computers. They will then format your resume for storage or scanning, and enter it into a tracking system that performs candidate searches.

When employers and recruiters have a job to fill, they will search their resume databases using certain keywords. The trick is in making sure that you have the right keywords on your resume so that the computer recognizes you as a good job candidate for that position.

Keywords are nouns, phrases, numbers, and industry-related jargon that highlight skill areas, achievements, and other professional qualities that match specific hiring requirements.

Choosing Your Keywords

The keywords that an employer uses to define a particular position vary according to the specifics of the position being filled, the company, and the hiring manager. Since you, as a job seeker, often have no way of knowing which keywords the employer will use, it isn't always easy to know which keywords to use on your resume. The best way to manage this is to simply write your resume in the best traditional form, focusing on action verbs, skills, special accomplishments, and results. After you've written your resume to say exactly *what* you want it to and in just the *way* you want it to, you can then read through it to identify your strategic keywords.

Some resume writers prefer to identify a list of about 20 keywords from the text of the resume and highlight them under the summary in a section marked "Keywords." As long as you have enough space to do this without overcrowding your resume, it can't hurt to ensure that the scanner catches all your keywords this way.

When answering newspaper job ads or other written position descriptions, use the job requirements listed in the ad to help you formulate your list of keywords to include in your resume.

Keyword Examples:

Here are some examples of the keywords employers might choose for certain positions.

Systems Analyst

- Systems Engineer
- Systems Analyst
- Software Engineer
- Analyzing
- Creating Specifications
- Installing
- CICS
- IDMS-ADSO
- IBM 43XX
- IBM50XX
- IDCAMS
- VSAM
- TSO/ISPF
- Writing
- Designing
- Troubleshooting
- Maintaining
- Training
- Certified Trainer
- BS, Mathematics & Computer Science

MIS Manager

- Program Management
- Program Administration
- Implementation
- Manufacturing Information System
- Budget
- Planning Systems
- Task Management
- Quality Control
- Government Contract Standards
- Implementation Team
- Long-range Planning
- Real-time Manufacturing Information System
- Real-time Material Control System
- Industrial Engineering
- Operations Analysis
- Engineer
- Supervising
- Directing
- Liaison
- MBA

Officer Manager

- Organizing
- Leading
- Supervising
- Problem-solving Abilities
- Multitasking
- Budget Coordination
- Written and Oral Communication Skills
- Accounts Receivable

- Accounts Payable
- Fast-paced Environment
- Deadlines
- Vendor Relations
- Negotiating
- Word
- Spreadsheet Development
- Scheduling

 Do not submit multiple resumes with varying versions of your work history in an attempt to hit more keyword targets. Your resume will lose all credibility with any employer who notices the variations.

YOUR ELECTRONIC RESUME

On occasion, an employer might give you the opportunity to submit your resume electronically. This is usually a second choice to sending a hard copy; with electronic resumes you have limited control over the appearance of your resume, because it goes through *their* word processor and is printed on *their* paper. In some cases, however, a company specifies that an electronic resume is preferred.

If you choose to send your resume electronically, be sure to find out the employer's electronic submission requirements. They should specify one or more file formats in which to save your resume file.

The two most common file formats used are ASCII (American Standard Code for Information Interchange) and RTF (Rich Text Format).

ASCII

Because of its simplicity, ASCII text enables job seekers to construct an online resume that any prospective employer can retrieve and read, no matter what kind of computer they are using.

 ASCII is a standard, common text language that enables different word processing applications to read and display the same text information. It is the simplest form of text, and it has no formatting mechanism.

The advantage of ASCII files is that they are recognized universally and they cut down significantly on unloadable file incidents. The disadvantage is that, because they carry no formatting information, your resume might arrive looking like an encrypted secret message so that the employer has to sort through a confusing maze of words to get to the needed information.

 You might consider sending a hard copy of your resume as well as the electronic version as insurance against transmission errors or problems with uploading.

To minimize the encryption effect, watch for these common mistakes:

- **Using special characters** Characters, such as mathematical symbols and quotation marks, do not get accurately transferred in the text save. AVOID them!
- **Using tabs** Tabs do not translate well on ASCII documents. You must use your spacebar instead of the tab key to inset any portion of your resume.
- **Poor alignment** Use a flush left margin of 0, with a right margin of 65. This left-justified format is preferred for scanning resumes and online viewing.

- **Fancy fonts** Remember that fonts will become whatever a computer uses as its default face and size so bolding, underlining, italics, and varied font sizes should not be included in your ASCII resume. Type in Courier font.

- **Wrapping words** Use hard carriage returns to insert line breaks as you compose your electronic resume. Do not use your word-wrap feature!

- **Spelling errors** As with any resume, spelling errors are deadly! Check your document and proofread it carefully before you save it as a text file.

- **Save it!** Don't forget that after you've constructed your ASCII resume, you can save this file and cut and paste it anywhere on the Web! And, if employers request that you forward your resume in ASCII text via e-mail, you will have the document ready to send.

RTF Files

RTF files are recognized by popular word processors, such as MS Word and WordPerfect. They have an advantage over ASCII in that they carry formatting information. Be aware, however, that a word processor different from your own might do some undesirable redecorating of your resume.

E-Mail

When sending your resume directly to an employer using e-mail, follow these steps to ensure that your resume arrives safely:

1. Obtain the electronic submission requirements before e-mailing your resume to an employer.

2. Be sure to type your resume on a word processor that allows you to save in the format you need.

3. Save your resume, and then attach it to the e-mail letter you will use as a cover letter (see Chapter 20, "Cover Letters").

4. Before sending your resume to the employer, consider sending it to yourself or someone you know who has the word processor the employer uses. Open it and see how it will look when they receive and print it.

5. Send it to the employer, making sure that you have the correct address.

CHAPTER SUMMARY

In this chapter, you learned to write your resume so that employers can scan and search it effectively. You also learned about electronic resumes and sending them by e-mail.

CHAPTER 18

Resumes on the Web

In this chapter, you will learn about the job search and resume services that the Web has to offer, and how to use them effectively.

USING THE WEB

The art of conducting a job search hasn't been the same since the Web came into popular use. No longer is a job search limited to whom you know or what you can read in the classified job ads. The Web abounds with opportunities to connect with other job seekers and with employers, to explore career possibilities across the globe and to research opportunities and companies that interest you.

To begin your Web adventure, try using the keyword "Resume" to search the Web. This will give you a broad picture of what job search choices the Web has in store for you. You will find these possibilities and more:

- You can peruse the booths at virtual job fairs in any location and forward your resume to the companies there.

- You can use a personal job shopper service that will browse a database of jobs for you, and then automatically e-mail any matches to your address.

- You can post a home-page resume that advertises your skills online and allows you to receive e-mail or an instant message from other job seekers or potential employers.

- You can ask for the advice of career experts about your own particular career issues.

- You can now even add video to your online resume so that prospective employers can see and hear you talking about your career credentials.

 The possibilities are exciting, and the opportunities great, but don't get so caught up in using the Web that you neglect your other job search methods!

There are three popular Web options that you should be sure to take a look at as you begin your job search.

Online Resume Services

Online resume services are often huge career sites full of information useful to anyone searching for a job or just beginning the career exploration process. They usually provide company profiles, recent articles, and job search tips, as well as information on writing resumes.

Some resume services ask you to use their online resume form, which then gets entered into a searchable database. Most allow you to post your resume free of charge, and they give you a password to allow you private access. Employers are usually charged a fee to post their job openings with these services, which you are given the opportunity to peruse for free. Employers usually must also pay a fee to get access to the resume database, or to have a search conducted for them along specified criteria.

Some resume services ask you to use their online form to submit your resume, and some even provide a field for a cover letter. Do some browsing through a few resume sites to get a feel for how the game is played.

To Post or Not to Post?

Consider the following when deciding whether to post your resume online:

- Would the employers you hope to attract be likely to search the database you are using to post your resume?

- Will your resume remain confidential on this system?

- Will this service showcase your resume exclusively?
- Does this database allow your resume to shine, or is there a better way to get a particular employer's attention?
- Does the database to which you're submitting your resume post the types of jobs you are interested in and qualified for?
- How long will your resume stay on this system?

 The posting process is not always confidential. Consider this as you contemplate posting.

Company Web Sites

A discussion of electronic resumes would be incomplete without mentioning the excellent job search tool of monitoring company Web sites.

Hiring managers and recruiters are finding the Web to be a quick and inexpensive source for employment advertising, accessible 24 hours a day. More and more companies are relying on their own Web sites to post jobs and attract job applicants.

You will find that most large American corporations and organizations have their own Web sites, and a good percentage of these post current job openings there. Many allow you to submit a resume electronically in response to a particular opening.

But using company Web sites forces you to do a little career focus work up front. If you allow yourself to wander aimlessly through company Web pages, you can quickly become distracted and overwhelmed by the vast array of choices. You need to know what you'd like to do and where you'd like to do it, before browsing Web sites becomes worthwhile!

Company Web Sites Worth Watching

Try these hot company Web sites that post job openings and offer the applicant a chance to submit online resumes:

www.gecareers.com An excellent, extensive site full of information on the General Electric corporation, including job postings and a chance to submit your resume online via e-mail. It also offers detailed information on submitting an ASCII resume.

www.ibm.com   Has a job match system that will match your resume against current jobs or those available within six months. You can choose to write a resume using their electronic form or send your own resume using ASCII.

www.tectronix.com   Has an online response form that you fill out in response to particular job postings. You can also send a non-targeted resume to be considered for future possibilities. It also offers detailed information on sending a scannable resume.

www.microsoft.com   Promises to keep your resume active for up to a year. It also allows you to build a resume onto their form or send one electronically using ASCII.

www.xerox.com   Asks you to paste your resume into their system. It offers detailed corporate information and extensive job postings.

The Top Job and Resume Sites

Several hot spots dominate the world of Web career sites. No job seeker today is doing a thorough exploration of today's career possibilities without checking into these amazing sites. Here are four of them:

www.careermosaic.com   An extensive site that covers all the angles of the job search, from online job fairs, company Web sites, and job postings, to a free resume posting service. Note that they do charge a fee to potential employers who want to view candidates' resumes, however.

www.monster.com   An excellent place to search job postings, research companies, chat with other job seekers, or read up on the latest career happenings. You can even have your resume reviewed and critiqued by a professional. This site lists nearly 250,000 job opportunities.

www.jobbankusa.com   Provides employment and resume information services to job candidates, employers, and recruitment firms. It also offers a free resume posting service.

www.careerpath.com   A Web page put together by the newspaper affiliates that offers everything from chat rooms and recent career articles, to a resume posting service.

Other Resume and Job Search Hot Spots

You can also try these impressive job sites:

www.careermart.com

www.careerbuilder.com

www.ajb.dni.us.com (America's Job Bank)

www.joboptions.com

www.careerweb.com

www.headhunter.net

www.careerShop.com

www.getajob.com

Specialized Resume and Job Sites

The following sites cater to the needs of particular categories of job seekers.

Experienced Professionals:

www.topjobsusa.com

www.hotjobs.com

Federal Jobs:

www.usajobs.opm.gov

www.federaljobs.net

www.fedjobs.com

Students/Recent Graduates:

www.jobdirect.com

www.jobtrak.com

Equal Employment Opportunity:

www.black-collegian.com

IT/Technical Jobs:

www.careermarthi-tech.com

www.topjobsusa.com

Temporary Jobs:

www.net-temps.com

Healthcare:

www.healthcareerweb.com

Military:

www.corporategrayonline.com

There are many more job and resume sites on the Web. The possibilities are endless! Take the time to explore them and watch the electronic world of job searching unfold before you!

CHAPTER SUMMARY

In this chapter, you learned about online resume services, and explored the job search possibilities that the Web provides.

CHAPTER 19

Letters of Reference and Recommendation

In this chapter, you learn how to collect a list of references and letters of recommendation that will impress a potential employer.

REFERENCE LISTS

A reference list is a prepared list of the names of colleagues, business associates, and friends who know you well and who are willing to give you a glowing recommendation to an interested employer.

Although job seekers no longer refer to their reference list on the resume itself, you should still have this list carefully prepared and available in case it is requested during your job search.

When writing your list, include three to six names of people who would be willing to speak with a potential employer about your positive personal and professional attributes. Be sure to choose people who know about your accomplishments and who will give you enthusiastic praise!

The Keys to Producing an Impressive Reference List

- Get permission from every person you plan to include on your list before you begin.

- Be sure to write your name and telephone number at the top of your reference list. If it somehow becomes separated from your resume, it can still be identified as yours.

- Choose former bosses, coworkers, professional associates, or people of status in the community who can attest to your professional integrity and effectiveness.

- Your list might include family friends or neighbors who are willing to attest to your excellent character. However, you should use no more than two non-business acquaintances on a list of five or more references.

- List each name with an address, phone number, and job title (or descriptive title).

- Your list should be neat, error-free, and centered neatly on the page.

- It should be typed in a font that matches your resume font.

- The paper for your reference list should match your resume paper.

Bring several copies of your reference list with you to all interviews. Be sure to offer it to the employer at the end of the interview, if he or she hasn't already requested it. Don't, however, pull it from your briefcase and hand it to him or her without first being asked to do so. Simply alert the employer that you have brought one with you and that you would be happy to let him or her have one if he or she would like to see it.

 Make sure that every person you have chosen as a reference knows that he or she was included on your list! Neglecting to do this can make for a hesitant or reluctant reference, which might cause you to lose the job offer.

Sample Reference List

```
Reference List For:
PATTI RESTICK
(410) 555 2916

Dr. Paul Mechstein, President
Summerville and Mechstein, Inc.
12116 Bright Place
Columbia, MD  21044
(410) 555-7869

Shiela Chaker, Lab Director
Siena Biotech
1344 Technology Place
Fort Worth TX  22377
(619) 555-9080

Cleo Lichten, Associate Professor
Biology Department
Northland College
Ashland, WI  55212
(719) 555-3065

Lee Westgate, Owner
Westgate Financial
6 Plaza Center
Columbia, MD  21044
(410) 555-9774
```

LETTERS OF RECOMMENDATION

Occasionally, you are asked to supply an employer with a letter of recommendation. Or, you might simply want to request one from a trusted
manager or colleague to use throughout your job search. Follow these
guidelines as you consider a letter of recommendation:

- When asking a person to write a letter of recommendation, give them
  a specific time when you need the letter to be completed.

    Try to allow about two weeks for completion. Leaving the com-
    pletion date open-ended creates the possibility of embarrassment on
    both sides if it hasn't been written and you have to keep asking for it.

- Give the person a copy of your resume or a list of your skills to use
  when writing the letter.

    Even if you have worked closely with the person and you think he
    or she is already familiar with your skills and accomplishments, he
    or she will appreciate having your resume to refresh his or her
    memory.

- If you are sending the recommendation letter in response to a specific job opening, give the letter writer a copy of the job listing, if possible.

  This allows the writer to tailor the letter to address the employer's needs.

- Write a thank-you note to each person who took the time to prepare a letter for you.

  If they can take the time out of their busy day to do you a favor, it is important for you to show your appreciation. Remember, this person might also be called upon to give you a verbal recommendation!

OTHER LETTERS TO HAVE READY

As your job search begins, think of any other written praise you might have received throughout your professional experience. These can include:

- Positive performance reviews
- Letters from bosses or supervisors in praise of a particular project you were associated with
- Thank-you letters from clients for excellent service

Make plenty of legible copies of these letters and bring them with you to interviews throughout your job search.

 Do not attach these letters to the resume itself. Most employers do not appreciate receiving paperwork they didn't request.

CHAPTER SUMMARY

In this chapter, you learned how to use letters of reference, recommendation, and praise to make a positive impression on potential employers.

CHAPTER 20

Cover Letters

In this chapter, you learn the steps to creating a great cover letter, and the dos and don'ts of successful letters that land interviews.

WHAT DO COVER LETTERS DO?

Cover letters originated as a polite introduction to the resume, a "thanks for reading the attached resume" letter. But a good cover letter is more complex than this: It should not only serve as an introduction, but also as an opportunity to grab the hiring manager's attention and keep it.

Good Cover Letters Give Good Clues

The importance of a well-written cover letter has grown in recent years. Today's unstable job market has created a much higher volume of consistent hiring activity throughout the corporate world, bringing an increased risk of costly turnover. Employment managers, looking for as many clues as possible to a potential hire's personality, behavioral skills, and technical abilities, now look beyond the resume to the cover letter for answers. Employers screen cover letters for these things:

- **Writing ability** Your letter won't make it past the first glance if it isn't written well, with good grammar and no spelling errors. A well-written letter indicates intelligence, attention to detail, and conscientiousness.

- **Choice of content** The employer will look for the writer to make a logical presentation of skills and to stick to the point without a lot of rambling.

- **Skills and qualities that match their needs** The bottom line: Your letter must immediately convince the reader that you have what he or she wants.

- **Personality indicators** The employer needs to know that you can tow the line when the going gets tough. He or she needs to know that you can work well as a team member and take initiative when your position calls for leadership. These types of personality indicators are the things a good cover letter is made of.

THE COVER LETTER, SECTION BY SECTION

Ms. Samantha Binda
Vice President, Corporate Communications
SouthEast Industries
35 International Center
Richmond, VA 40597

Dear Ms. Binda:

The Charlottesville Gazette ran a fascinating series of articles recently on SouthEast's decision to set up a corporate communications center in Charlottesville. As a longtime resident of the Charlottesville area, I'm confident you'll be more than pleased with your new association with our friendly city.

The articles offered many complimentary insights into the SouthEast corporate structure, and even mentioned your election last year into the Top Twenty list for best-managed small companies in the Mid-Atlantic region. The article, as you may have read, heralded the arrival of SouthEast's corporate offices as the beginning of a strong new growth era for both Charlottesville and SouthEast. As an experienced corporate communications professional, I would like to be a part of SouthEast's exciting new direction.

The newspaper series mentioned your strong new emphasis on public relations. With over 8 years experience in public relations for a mid-size manufacturing firm, I feel I could bring a knowledge of the local media and an expertise in small/mid-size public relations to your new team at SouthEast in Charlottesville. My expertise includes:

- Ten years experience in corporate communications, with 3 years as Assistant Director of Public Relations.

- Extensive experience in Charlottesville-area media relations, with excellent results in significant and positive news coverage.

- Solid background in executive interview preparation and spokesperson responsibilities.

- Varied writing experience that includes news releases, financial and consumer collateral, speeches, and development of video and slide presentations.

I am enthusiastic about the possibility of putting my expertise to use for an emerging, dynamic company like SouthEast. I will follow up with you later in the week to explore the potential opportunities at your new corporate communications center here in Charlottesville. I look forward to talking with you soon.

Sincerely,

Justin Dillon

The Opening

The cover letter must open with an attention-grabber! In the preceding example, the first sentence keeps the reader's attention by mentioning an article that the potential employer has probably read and is proud of. The employer will want to continue reading your letter to find out what you have to say about the article and his company.

The Body

In the body of the letter, your main thrust is to convince the employer that you are the person for the job. Identify what it is you'd like to do for the company, and tell them why you consider yourself the best person to do it. Cite specific examples of your qualifications for the position you seek, including particular accomplishments and the results you achieved. Do not merely list the very same accomplishments that you have chosen for your resume: expand on the positives in your resume and offer more.

 Keep the tone of the letter upbeat and confident.

The Closing

In closing your letter, take the responsibility for future action upon yourself. Don't be timid: Tell the reader that you will call to set up a time for an interview. Then, of course, you must do as you said and make the call! Before closing the letter, thank the hiring manager for his time.

SEVEN STEPS TO A GREAT COVER LETTER

A cover letter should generate attention and interest. It should make the prospective employer curious to know more about you, and it should make him or her want to meet you in person for a face-to-face interview. This is no small feat, considering the sea of cover letters that cross the desk of most employment managers in a typical day. How do you make yours stand out?

1. **Make it brief and to the point**   One page only, please. No rambling, meandering, or long-winded recitations on the state of the job market, industry fluctuations, and the like. The reader wants to know whether you are qualified for the job: Tell the reader that, and nothing else.

2. **It must be directed to the specific company or job; it is NOT a generalized letter**   Your letter shouldn't look like the exact same one you sent to 20 other companies, with the name and date changed

at the top. An employer can spot a phony formula letter 100 miles away, and won't bother reading it because he or she knows it can't have anything pertinent to say. Do your research to make your letter address the particular needs of the company!

3. **Address it to a specific person** Never write a letter "To Whom It May Concern:" Always do your homework to find out the name of the person who has the power to hire you (NOT a personnel representative, but the hiring manager himself). If you don't already know the name, call the company and ask!

4. **It must be an attention-grabber!** Letters that start out poorly never get the chance to shine later because they get ditched before they get finished. Those dull, stilted cover letters are a dime a dozen, and not worth reading. That first sentence has got to be a doozy!

5. **Write it carefully** Most employers I know will use an obvious spelling or grammatical error as an "automatic out policy." If they see one, the letter gets pitched. Period. Computer scanners, by the way, can be just as ruthless.

6. **Write it neatly** Use $8^1/2" \times 11"$ paper that matches the resume bond and color. Type and print it to make a professional presentation.

7. **Offer specifics** Vague referrals to "superior results" or "excellent skills" tend to not ring true and can portray you as desperate, boastful, or unsure of your direction. In order to impress, accomplishments and skills must be spelled out specifically and quantified whenever possible.

 You can use bullets to highlight your accomplishments within the body of the letter.

THREE COVER LETTERS THAT GET RESULTS

Three styles of cover letter have proven themselves to be especially effective in different situations. They are: cover letters in response to job ads, targeted cover letters, and referral letters.

The Cover Letter in Response to an Ad

Advertisements for open positions offer an outstanding opportunity to write a terrific cover letter. Why? Because in most cases, the ad tells you exactly what qualifications the employer is seeking! You can craft your cover letter to address the specific needs of the employer, using the eye-catching two-column approach. Set your cover letter up like this:

Chase Winkler
Tri-state Plastics, Inc.
4114 Westdale Ave.
Cincinnati, OH 45089

Dear Mr. Winkler,

This responds to your advertisement for the Director of Marketing position for Tri-state Plastics. As you can see, my background and skills are an excellent match for your requirements:

Your Requirements	My Qualifications
5 Years Management Experience	6 Years Marketing Management at City Product Works, Inc.
Experience in Strategic Planning	Created 5 year segmented market plan for consumer houseware product line, which resulted in profit increase of 30% over non-segmented plan.
Budget Planning	Managed budget of 10MM
Strong oral and written communication skills	Wrote business plans and presented proposals to Leadership team and top level clients. Lead meetings and conference workshops.
Proven ability to lead and motivate employees	Best retention/promotion record at City Product Works.
Preferred MBA degree	MBA, Miami University, Oxford Ohio

There are other areas of accomplishment in my background which may be of interest to you. I will call you early next week to discuss the possibility of a personal meeting. Or, you are welcome to reach me at 765-4638.

Sincerely,

Taylor Garricks

Notice how the letter focuses only on the specific matches between what you have to offer and what the hiring manager wants. Hiring managers will appreciate this style of letter and will be impressed with your attention to their needs.

The introductory and closing sentences should match the tone of the ad-response letter: to the point and frills-free.

The Targeted Cover Letter

In some cases you might want to send resumes and cover letters to companies that appeal to you but that don't have any specific job openings that you are aware of. Here, you are trying simply to get your foot in the door, to stir up their interest in you and let them know you have interest in them.

With this type of cover letter (called a *targeted* cover letter because you are targeting a particular company), you don't have that great advantage of a written ad, which spells out job qualifications for you. But if you are a smart job seeker, you can still tailor your letter to address an employer's specific needs. How? By doing a little research!

Employers are always impressed and flattered by a job seeker who has done his or her homework well enough to recognize the needs of the organization that he or she is writing to. Your cover letter, which targets the current trends and particular needs of a company, will stand heads above the multitude of predictable, formulaic letters that pile up daily upon their desks.

Let's say that the company you want to send your resume to is XYZ Inc, a company with an attractive building that you have noticed while driving on Highway 64. You know very little about the company except what you've heard by word of mouth: that they make widgets, that they've been in business for about 20 years, and that they have been growing steadily for the past five years. How do you find out more about them?

- **The Internet** Look up the company Web page to learn amazing amounts of information, from historical to financial. It might mention new products, recent acquisitions or expansions, or the company vision statement. If you don't know their Web address, call the receptionist and find out!

- **Written articles** You might look in trade journals, newspapers, or magazines for articles relating to the company itself or the industry as a whole. If you don't know how to find them yourself, ask a reference librarian at your local library. They tend to be very resourceful in digging up the information you want.

- **Reference books** In the Reference section of your local library, look for the business books that contain profiles of various types of companies. A couple to start with might be Dun and Bradstreet's Million Dollar Directory or Moody's Manuals.

How to Write Your Research Knowledge into the Letter

Now that you've done your research, you need to make sure the employer knows the work you've done right up front. It should scream for attention in the very first sentence. Study the following example:

Ms. Janet Wilson
XYZ, Inc.
4 Fripp Square
Ashland, WI 56069

Dear Ms. Wilson:

I read the recent article in *Business Week* about the Widget Industry's expansion into new markets, especially in the local geographic sector. I was impressed by the special mention that XYZ received for your innovative new designs and cutting-edge technology.

I have a great deal of expertise in Widget design and fabrication, and am writing to see if there might be an opportunity for me to contribute to XYZ as you grow into new market sectors.

My background includes:

- 10 years in Widget design, including specifications and regulations.
- Technical expertise in E-glass, S-glass, and conventional resins.
- 6 Years supervising technical teams in design and fabrication.
- An excellent record of deadline management and cost control.

I received invaluable hands-on training in Widget design and fabrication by working for a small start-up Widget firm, A.B. Edwards, in Roanoke, VA. After 4 years there, I moved to Trenton, New Jersey, where I supervised a Technical Design and Quality Control team of 12 . I am proud to say our team won consistent praise and several corporate awards for outstanding work.

I will follow up with you early next week to see if my background and skills might be of use to XYZ at this time of growth. Or, you may contact me at 759-9087. I would value the opportunity to talk with you.

Sincerely Yours,

Kiera Morgan

The Referral

Another excellent way to catch a reader's attention is to mention the name of someone that he or she knows in the first sentence. Dropping a name in the first sentence obligates the reader to continue on, in case an action or response is necessary. The name will preferably refer to a colleague or associate that the potential employer knows and respects.

 If you lack a powerful name, try using a name of anyone connected to the company, even if the reader won't immediately recognize it. Seeing any name at the top of the letter will still obligate him or her to read on, just in case.

Study the following example:

Ms. Jacqueline Schauer
Executive Vice President
ELK Publishing Affiliates
Gary, IN 65471

Dear Ms. Schauer:

Russell Lili, an associate of mine who has worked with you on a recent project for CBC, suggested that I write to you about the position you may soon have available in marketing management.

Throughout my tenure in the marketing arena, I have read and heard consistently positive reports about ELK's innovative management culture and vision for growth. After 8 years of progressively responsible supervisory marketing experience, I am well prepared to move into a marketing management position, and I am eager to become a part of such a forward-thinking team.

My background has focused on publishing promotions and direct marketing. My early career was spent in New York City with Time, Inc., where I served in a number of marketing assignments including promotions supervisor for a start-up magazine called "Sleuth". Since 1996, I have held supervisory positions in the corporate direct marketing group at Kirkland Publishing in Chicago.

Russell felt that I should contact you immediately, since my unique blend of direct marketing knowledge and expertise in the publishing world are a strong fit with the needs that ELK anticipates.

I will call you in a few days to see if we might arrange a meeting where we could discuss the possibilities in more detail. Or, you may reach me at 555-7590. I look forward to talking with you soon.

Sincerely,

Lorraine Willows

DOS AND DON'TS FOR COVER LETTERS

DO Be sure to include a phone number in your cover letter so an employer can reach you if he or she wishes.

DON'T List hobbies or personal interests in your cover letter, unless they are directly relevant to the position or the company.

DO Keep a copy of each cover letter you write for your records. This way you can follow up on those phone calls you promised to make.

DON'T Use a sexist salutation, such as "Dear Sir:", or "Gentlemen:". Remember, find the name of the person who has hiring power and use that name. If you are answering a blind box number from a job ad and can't find the name, try addressing the letter to "Dear Boxholder:".

DON'T Include a salary history or salary expectations in the cover letter! Even if a job ad requests that you do so, do not list an exact salary, because this puts you in a poor negotiating position at offer time. If you feel you must address the salary in the cover letter because of a specific and strongly worded request, be as vague as possible with exact figures. Either give no figure at all, as in "I am flexible in terms of salary", or speak in terms of ranges, as in, "My most recent salary was in the $40K–$50K range."

DO Follow formal business letter rules when writing a paragraph-style cover letter. Use extreme block style (all parts starting at the left margin), or modified block (heading, closing, and signature centered, the rest left-margin). Keep side, top, and bottom margins at least one inch.

DON'T Use excessive abbreviations or acronyms. For the most formal presentation, all words should be spelled out.

DO Use a traditional letter closing, such as "Sincerely," or "Yours Truly." For something a little less formal, you might try "Cordially."

DON'T Write your current job title after your name in the closing of your letter. You are not writing the cover letter on behalf of your present employer.

It works against you at the negotiation table to list your salary expectations or salary history in the cover letter! Avoid all mention of salary if possible.

CHAPTER SUMMARY

In this chapter, you learned three types of cover letters that get results, and how to use cover letters to impress potential employers that you are the person for the job.

CHAPTER 21

The Job Search

In this chapter, you learn to use four proven job search strategies and to open doors to job opportunities through networking and information meetings.

ARMED AND READY

Now that you've armed yourself with an impressive resume and a tailored cover letter, you are ready to explore the vast new world of job possibilities!

Before plunging in to your search, consider these points:

- The key to a successful job search is not how hard you work, but how *smart* you work.

- Job search success is not found in the quantity of resumes you send out, but in the *quality* of the contacts you make.

- You will not find success by letting the winds of fate blow you to and fro. A job search becomes successful when you take control of the sail and set it against the wind to steer yourself where you want to go.

- Successful job search strategies aren't for the faint of heart. Wimps and weaklings beware! You must be decisive, take risks, get gutsy, and persevere!

- A rejection doesn't mean that you aren't good enough. Sometimes rejection just happens, whether rightly or wrongly. Remember, the Beatles were rejected by the first record companies they approached!

THE JOB MARKET

The job market consists of the constant, ongoing efforts of potential employers and active job seekers working diligently to find each other. Employers use a variety of tactics to try to locate and hire talented people, and job seekers work equally hard trying to track down employers with good job opportunities.

The job market is in a constant state of flux as new positions open and others close. Job possibilities can open when:

- Employees are promoted
- Employees are transferred to a new location
- Employees retire
- Companies expand
- New industries emerge
- Older industries change form
- Companies merge or reorganize

 You are not alone! Each year, almost 20 percent of all working people find themselves engaged in a job or career change.

PROVEN JOB SEARCH STRATEGIES

A job search campaign should be conducted on several different fronts. By spreading your net wider, you cover more territory and become exposed to a much broader variety of job possibilities.

Your chances of employment increase with the number of job opportunities you explore. Don't settle for a narrow job search!

There are four proven areas that should be woven together to form the focus of your job search efforts: perusing the published market, targeting companies, using recruiters and agencies, and working your contacts.

Perusing the Published Market

Throughout your search, keep an eye on all newspapers and related periodicals for new positions popping up. Answer any ads that seem to be a good fit with what you have to offer. Look for a 70 to 80 percent match of the ad's stated job requirements with your qualifications.

Don't always look for ads with a 100 percent match— you are likely to be overqualified for these jobs, because they leave you with no room to grow.

Tips for Answering Ads

- Read the ad carefully to distinguish between what is required and what is merely a desired quality. Much of what appears in an ad is "wish list" material, and not necessary for a potential match.
- The qualities listed at the top of the ad tend to be the most important qualities for the job. When answering the ad, list those qualities first.
- Be sure to use the two-column cover letter as described in chapter 20.
- Don't re-write your resume in response to every ad. The cover letter should handle any specifics you want to highlight for each particular opening.
- If the ad is a blind box number with no indication of company name, it is wise to make an attempt to discover the identity of the boxholder. If it is through the post office (as opposed to a newspaper box), call the post office that handles that address and ask for the name of

the boxholder. If they won't give it to you, cite the Freedom of Information Act.

- Don't expect a huge response. The typical response rate for an answered job ad is less than 10 percent, so don't get discouraged if you don't hear back. It's just part of the game.

 Don't forget to check company Web sites: This is a cost-conscious way for companies to spread the word about employment opportunities. See chapter 18 for more details.

Requests for Salary Information

Many ads request that you supply them with a "salary history" or "salary expectation." This is a no-win situation for you. Consider this:

- If you list a salary that is higher than they wanted to pay, you price yourself out of the job before you even get a chance to interview. The screeners might just toss your nice resume in the trash.
- If you list a salary that is too low, you might still get the job offer, but at a much lower salary than they might have otherwise paid.

So how do you avoid their questions?

Be as vague as possible, and avoid mentioning salary altogether if you feel you can get away with it. Never reveal your dollar-for-dollar salary history, and always speak in terms of salary ranges. Suggestions include:

- If the ad asks for salary expectations, say this: "My salary expectations are flexible." (There will be time to negotiate your terms later. For now, you simply want to make it to the interview).
- If the ad asks for salary history, say this: "My salary history has been consistently progressive as I have been promoted to increasingly responsible positions."
- If the ad INSISTS upon specific details of your salary, use ranges to give yourself a broader chance of being within the parameters they are looking for. Use a range of about $10K, such as, "My salary expectations are in the $30K to $40K range."

Do not let your low-end figure be any lower than your absolute bottom-line salary that you'd accept for that job.

 Only about 15 percent of all jobs are found through published job ads. Don't limit your job search to reading job ads alone

Targeting Companies

A great way to take control of your job search is by writing out a list of companies that strike you as good places to work. Start with a list of about 20 "dream" companies that appeal to you. Consider these questions:

- Is the company location appealing?
- Do you feel comfortable with the size of the company?
- Do you enjoy the corporate setting?
- How is the corporate culture there?
- Does the industry match your skills and needs?
- Does the company seem poised for growth?
- Does the company enjoy a good reputation?
- Would the company offer opportunities for professional growth, travel, and so on?
- Is the industry and company solid and strong?
- Is the company known for shake-ups, such as mergers, acquisitions, or downsizings?

After targeting 20 top companies, your research phase begins. Use the Internet or library reference books to locate the name of the hiring managers in the company department in which you'd like to work. Or, if you don't mind picking up a phone, try calling the main reception number, and ask for the head of the department that interests you. Before they connect you, get the name of the person with the correct spelling.

Use this information to address your targeted cover letters (see chapter 20) to the particular departments within the specific companies that appeal to you. This system has allowed you to zero in on your job search target with pinpoint accuracy, completely avoiding the screeners in Human Resources whose job it is to screen you out.

Using Recruiters and Agencies

 Going directly to the source of the job before the job is even published is a great way to unearth that hidden job market!

Many job seekers balk at the idea of using a recruiter or employment agency to help them in their job search. Some feel that these companies lack integrity, and that they are out to make a buck instead of find a satisfying job for their customers. Others don't like to turn over the control of their search to someone else.

Using recruiters can be a positive experience, though, as long as you are savvy to the way the system works. It can be a great way to get the inside scoop on positions that might not be advertised to the general public. Best of all, it's usually free of charge, so what do you have to lose? Follow these guidelines to using recruiters successfully:

- **Never pay a fee to a recruiter, unless you are a first-time job seeker** In most cases, the hiring company pays the service fee, not the job seeker. Don't ever pay a fee up front!

- **Don't give exclusivity to any firm** Some recruiters ask you to sign a form which gives them the right to work with you exclusively. Don't sign it: Let as many recruiters help you in your job search as you can get!

- **Never tell a recruiter where you have interviewed,** Otherwise, they can use this information to send other people out for that job, which can hurt your chances of getting hired.

- **Make use of specialized firms** Many recruiters specialize in a certain industry, such as accounting, technical, or administrative work. These firms tend to have the most thorough knowledge of the companies that hire in these areas.

How to Find a Good Recruiter

There are three types of recruiters: employment agencies, contingency search firms, and retainer firms. I've outlined each of the three below.

Employment Agencies

These tend to handle entry-level to middle-management–level positions. These agencies typically don't get paid unless they place someone. Employment agencies are usually listed in the local yellow pages.

 Because employment agencies work on commission, they aren't always concerned with the quality of the match between candidate and employer. Be cautious about the jobs you might be offered.

Contingency Search Firms

Contingency firms tend to handle jobs in a higher salary range than employment agencies, and they have a lower volume of traffic. Therefore, their service can be more personalized, and more attention is paid to the quality of the job match. Still, contingency firms don't get paid until the placement is made, so be aware of your own needs when considering a job offer.

Retainer Firms

Retainer firms deal mostly with upper-level management positions in the higher salary ranges. These are the traditional "headhunters," who fill high-level positions for companies, and get paid on retainer. A thorough list of retainer firms and contingency firms across the nation can be found in *The Directory of Executive Recruiters*, which you can pick up in your local library.

After you have chosen a list of recruiters with whom you'd like to work, send them a letter and resume or call them by phone to see if you can schedule an appointment to see them. Recruiters often keep even unsolicited resumes on file to use in future job searches; therefore, don't give up if you don't get an immediate response.

Working Your Contacts

The fourth and by far the most successful way to go about a job search is simply to spread the word that you are in the market for a job. More than 70 percent of new jobs are found through word of mouth. Talk to the people you know and the people they know; your network of contacts will grow and broaden.

Anyone and everyone is an eligible network contact. Your neighbors, friends at church, business associates, and anyone you have a conversation with!

Some people think that networking amounts to accosting everyone you meet with the plea, "I need a job. Do you know of one anywhere?" This is just the opposite of what effective networking is all about. Study these guidelines to effective networking:

- **Take charge** Phrase your questions so that you are in charge of the next step, not your listener. Don't say, "If you find out about any jobs in accounting, call me." Instead, say, "I'd appreciate it if you could get me the name of the hiring manager in your company's accounting department. I'll call you on Wednesday to get that from you. Thanks!"

- **Avoid vague requests** Don't merely ask a contact to "keep your ears open for any jobs that open up," or, "Let me know if you ever hear of anything." This is a nebulous request that the listener can easily ignore or forget about, and it will probably lead to nothing.

- **Ask for names, not jobs** Ask your networking contact for specific names of people you can contact. Don't ask, "Do you know of any jobs that are open?" Instead ask, "Do you know of anyone at your company that I might talk to as a new networking contact? How about a manager in the inside sales area?"

Ask focused, DIRECTED questions that lead your listener to easy answers.

 The goal of a networking question is to get the *name* of someone else to talk to, *not* to get a job offer. The job offers will follow as your list of contacts grows.

The Information Meeting

This chain of communication—someone you know refers you to someone they know, who refers you to someone *they* know—eventually leads to an information meeting.

 An information meeting is a place to exchange professional information, establish a solid networking relationship, and get exposure in the job market.

Such a meeting takes place when your network of contacts has lead you to a person who seems to have helpful information about your field and goals, and who has access to other contacts for you to explore. Simply explain that you are expanding your network and would appreciate a few minutes of his time. You might invite him to lunch or meet in his office.

An Information Meeting Agenda

Because you have requested that this meeting take place, you are in charge of the agenda. Follow these rules for a successful information meeting.

- Remember that the goal of the meeting is to gather other names for your network, *not* to get a job directly. Don't make a pest of yourself by asking if he or she knows of any open jobs. (If you impress him or her and he or she knows of any open job, he will probably tell you about it anyway.)

- Feel free to begin the meeting with a little small talk to establish rapport, but don't overdo it.

- Ease his discomfort by stating directly that you are not there to seek a job from him. You should let him know that you are in the job market, but your reason for seeing him is not to ask for a job. You might explain that you are doing a bit of "career exploration" before settling into your next position and that you are trying to meet new people in the industry to learn more and establish new contacts.

 In today's unsteady work world, people appreciate having a large web of contacts. Most people will welcome a chance to meet a fellow professional as a new contact of their own!

- Satisfy his curiosity with a brief overview of your background and skills, two minutes should cover it. Give him a quick career history sketch, with a specific accomplishment or two thrown in.
- Ask questions that are relevant to your objectives (*not* about job possibilities!). Steer the conversation around his area of expertise.
- At appropriate points throughout the meeting, or toward the end of the allotted time, ask for names of other people that he or she suggests you might talk to. Be specific about the kind of people you'd like to meet.
- Don't forget that it is up to you to bring the meeting to a close. Take no more than about 30 minutes of his time.
- Offer a resume so he or she has your name and phone number for future networking possibilities. Ask for a business card, and mention that you'd like to keep in touch.
- Follow up with a thank you note. If you have contacted any of the people that he or she recommended, let him or her know that.

 Networking is a two-way street. As you make new contacts with people, think about ways that you might help them in their career as well.

Networking creates wonderful job leads and cultivates a group of associates and contacts that you can call upon in other professional situations.

 Don't let your contacts run dry. Check in with them periodically so that the relationship stays current.

You will be surprised at how many job leads you will unearth by digging around. Although each networking contact might not lead to a specific job opening, you can feel quite sure that you are on the path to exciting job opportunities with each new contact you make!

CHAPTER SUMMARY

In this chapter, you learned to put the four most effective job search tools together to form a unique and thorough search strategy. You learned the art of networking, and the keys to leading a successful networking meeting.

Appendix

The following pages contain an additional six resume examples for you to review. Notice how relatively small differences in style, format, and placement make big differences in the overall tone of each resume.

Though you can draw inspiration from what these job seekers have done, remember that your resume is ultimately a unique creation. No one else will bring the exact set of accomplishments, skills, and experience to the table as you, so take pride in your uniqueness and experiment until you find the look that's right for you.

JOEL PERRYSON
75 McCourt Street
East Chester, OH 54096
(513) 555-9088
email: Jolper@Home.com

PROFILE

Dependable, hardworking Customer Service/Accounts Receivable Professional with six years experience in a large corporate setting. Known for diplomacy skills in dealing with both internal and external customers. Tackle problems with tenacity, and always follow through to resolution. Particular expertise includes:

- Accounts Receivable
- Customer Communications
- Arbitration

- Credit Collections
- Problem Solving
- Account Resolution

EXPERIENCE

SOUTHWEST TEXTILE GROUP, Moline, TX   1994-2000

Credit Associate   (1997-2000)

Reviewed customer accounts and determined credit worthiness. Resolved problems with customer accounts, and wrote collection letters or made telephone contact to reconcile inconsistencies.

- Alleviated all long-term outstanding debts, which brought about substantial revenue collection for the company.
- Tracked account information on computer, which allowed for more thorough and efficient account review.
- Established positive rapport with both internal and external customers, resulting in timely credit collection

Customer Service Representative (1994-1997)

Communicated with customers to resolve problems with orders. Wrote informative letters to customers regarding issues with accounts or orders. Acted as liaison with sales personnel and other internal departments to keep the appraised of customer issues.

- Received consistent compliments for patience and sensitivity to customer needs.
- Fostered interactive communication between company sales representatives and customers to maint an ongoing positive business relationship.

EDUCATION

Lakeland High School, Forest Ridge, IL   Diploma 1993

PROFESSIONAL TRAINING

- Word for Windows 6.0
- Excel
- Telelphone Skills Workshop
- Business Communications Workshop

PERSONAL

Treasurer, Greater Chicago Amateur Magicians Organization
Volunteer, Forest Ridge Hotline Helpers

KIERA WILSON

33 Brandy Lane
Columbus, WI 34098

Home(398) 750-9906
Office(398) 750-9801

SUMMARY

Quality Contol Supervisor with 10 years experience in assembly and production. Skilled in all areas of assembly daily operations. Known for attention to detail, conscientious attitude, and excellent mamagement skills. Expertise includes:

- Quality Control
- Product Redesign
- Machine Maintenance
- Production Scheduling
- Employee Training
- Budget Development

EXPERIENCE

SHEL-FLOR CORPORATION   1994-2000
Holkam, CA

Quality Control Supervisor (1996-2000)

Supervised daily operation of Assembly Division, including 16 Assemblers and 4 Floaters. Scheduled employees and usage of equipment to meet production schedules. Inspected assembly areas to ensure compliance with company and OSHA standards.

- Increased productivity efficiency from 70% to 90% by setting clear objectives and effective team management.
- Improved absenteeism from 15% to 5% by initiating program of employee intiiatives.
- Reduced scrap rate from 20% to 5% by organizing more effective product inspections.
- Acted as Manager of Assemby in manager's absence.

Quality Control Associate (1994-1996)

Inspected incoming materials and final products. Acted on changes in quality standards.

- Chosen "Associate of the Month" for 6 consecutive months.
- Maintained excellent relationship with Management Teamand Assemblers.
- Trained new employees on equipment usage and production scheduling.

MAKRO, INC.   1990-1994
Chelsea, CA

Expediter

Expedited parts flow including outsie vendors and in-house machine parts. Monitored and communicated inventory needs for three manufactufacturing divisions.

EDUCATION

Duluth Community College   Duluth, MN   AA Degree   1991

CHASE J. RUDYMAN
44 Garrick Drive
Baltimore, MD 20202
(410) 555-5757

SUMMARY:
Dependable and motivated Mortgage/Loan Specialist with strong record of accomplishments
in loan and mortgage administration. Known for efficiency, team work, and creativity.
Extensive background in:

- · Negotiating Repayments   · HUD compliance   · Financial Statements

- · Foreclosures   . Research   · Workout Programs

PROFESSIONAL EXPERIENCE:

FIRST ATLANTIC BANK   Portsmouth, Maine   (1994 - 1998)
(Formerly CLASSIC RESIDENTIAL MORTGAGE CORPORATION)

MORTGAGE/LOAN SPECIALIST 1996 - 1998
Assisted delinquent mortgagees by negotiating a repayment schedule to prevent
foreclosure. Developed workout programs for mortgagors to maintain compliance with
investors. Prepared HUD claims and related forms for delinquent borrowers. Evaluated
financial statements of borrowers to determine appropriate workout program
(modifications, short-sale, dad-in-lieu of foreclosure).

Selected Accomplishments:

- Achieved low percentage of foreclosure through careful evaluation and
  thorough research.
- 100% delinquency report was reduced by 50% monthly.
- Met all investor guidelines prior to deadlines.

MORTGAGE OFFICER 1994 - 1996
Provided counseling for delinquent mortgagees to bring mortgage payments current.
Researched information regarding delinquent borrowers through Credit Bureau Reports.
Managed first mortgage loans for FNMA, FHLMC, CDA, HUD.

Selected Accomplishments:

- Number one administrator four consecutive quarters
- Lowered delinquencies by 70% monthly.
- Promoted to Specialist position after only 18 months.

EDUCATION: Catonsville Community College   1992-1993
                  Business Coursework

MORGAN L. TAYLOR, CPA
6 Loreli Court, Friendship, NM 60606
(719) 555-0989
E-mail: Mortay@aol.com

PROFILE: Strategic and analytical Accountant and Management Professional with over 15 years of diverse accounting, finance, and systems experience. Strong motivator, implementor and educator with emphasis on presenting, training and development. Areas of expertise include:

•Financial Statements	•Curriculum Design
•Project Management	•Training and Development
•Systems Implementation	•Account Analysis
•Fixed Asset Management	•Seminars and Workshops

PROFESSIONAL EXPERIENCE:

KOHLBERG LABORATORIES, Creekfield, NM   (1988 - 1999)
Financial Systems Manager   1995 - 1999
Coordinated and drove financial system-related projects and acted as liaison between Information Technology Department and Finance while implementing, instituting, and upgrading automated systems that created an efficient and value added team environment.

- Installed automated sales and use tax system which significantly reduced state audits and non-compliance penalties
- Implemented Fixed Asset Management System in Cayey, Puerto Rico resulting in $4K favorable adjustment from $25MM asset base

  Implemented mission critical, automated time and attendance payroll system without compromising integrity of payroll checks

  Designed and developed curriculum to train operations associates on Fundamentals of   Basic Accounting and Finance

Financial Reporting Manager   1992 - 1995;
Financial Reporting Supervisor   1988 - 1992
Maintained financial records for parent company which was comprised of three Realty companies, three satellite manufacturing facilities, and Maryland based activities.

- Established and installed fixed asset management system which effectively consolidated all assets for five separate local divisions
- Developed training materials and taught users functionality and utilization of General Ledger system in order to properly perform month-end close
- Motivated Sales Implementation Team to remain committed and focused on successfully achieving goal of becoming fully operational within one year

EDUCATION: MBA, University of Santa Fe, Santa Fe, NM
                        BS, Accounting, Northern Ohio College, Trenton, OH
                        LICENSE: CPA, State of New Mexico

TECHNICAL SKILLS:

                        Personal Computer Systems and Applications: Windows, Microsoft Office,
                        Lotus SmartSuite, WordPerfect, Internet.

                        Application/Implementation Systems: Infinium Software (Software 2000),
                        Vertex Sales and Use Tax, Kronos Time & Attendance, CLR-Fast Tax for
                        Fixed Assets (PWFAMS), Best FAS Encore for Fixed Assets.

AFFILIATIONS/COMMUNITY LEADERSHIP:
American Institute of Certified Public Accountants
Maryland Association of Certified Public Accountants
Student Relations Committee, MACPA
Certified Lay Speaker

Kurt Lunn
85 Kingsgate Way
Molina,KS 41554
(670) 555-4265

Profile

Dedicated financial sales professional with four years experience in banking industry. Expertise includes:

- Sales Training
- Knowledge of bank products and federal compliance regulations
- Maintaining a high level of customer service
- Demonstrated high performance and organizational skills

Professional Experience

First Third Bank, Karper, KS   (1996-Present)

TeleSales Representative

Sold all bank products through extensive inbound and outbound telephone campaigns and referred prospective customers to Mortgage Corporation, Consumer Financial Services, and Insurance Services.

- Conducted telephone sales seminar which improved rapport with customers and strengthened the impact of sales call.
- Successfully converted over 45% of potential sales calls to sales.
- Assisted in the training of new TeleSales Representatives.
- Managed outbound follow-up list, which resulted in cross sell ratio of 2:25.

CitizensBank Corporation, Cleveland, OH   (1994-1996)

Telephone Sales Representative II

Sold retail loan and deposit products through extensive inbound telephone campaigns. Developed and imparted product information to representatives to insure accurate and concise information was provided to customers. Supervised staff of 60.

- Elected telephone sales representative of the month for October, 1994, February, March, and April 1995.
- Motivated employees to focus on customer service and sales orientation.
- Assisted with development of product knowledge training materials and operational manuals.
- Consistently attained at least 125% of sales goal.

Education

Business Courses, University of Kansas City, Kansas City, KS   (1996)

Company-Sponsored Courses

Service Excellence, Consumer Lending Module, and Cash Management Product Knowledge

Technical Skills

Proficiency using Merlin, ACAPS, Webster Class, Boss, M&I, Microsoft Word, WordPerfect for Windows 6.1, and Quattro Pro 6.0

CARL J. EMILSON
3567 Deer Meadow Court
Fort Wayne, IN 21240
(516) 555-4368

PROFILE

Senior Marketing Manager with extensive experience in personal life insurance. Proven leadership and interpersonal skills, in-depth professional knowledge and extensive planning experience. Progressively increased scope, responsibility, and authority. Recognized for regulatory knowledge and dealings with state agencies. Demonstrated knowledge of marketing, sales training, customer relations, budget planning and control. Strongly committed to ethical treatment of associates and customers. Accomplishments include:

- Directed field force through two successful mergers
- Developed marketing programs to enhance client relations and attract new customers
- Skillfully chaired three annual industry conventions
- Formulated and implemented work ethics program
- Designed and presented focused performance measures and skills training

---
PROFESSIONAL EXPERIENCE

PLAINS LIFE/HOME MUTUAL LIFE, Fort Wayne, IN   (1985-1998)

Vice President – Home Mutual Sales   (1998)
Executive Vice President – Marketing   (1987-1998)
Vice President Agencies   (1985-1987)
Directed the Home Mutual Sales Division operations in seven states. Spearheaded sales; designed, introduced, and implemented motivational programs; and directed recruiting, budgeting, and training of field force. Developed and implemented innovative marketing plan involving reasoned risk-taking and cost control.

SELECTED ACCOMPLISHMENTS:

- Directed turnaround in sales which generated 12% increase after 6 years of flat performance
- Successfully managed field organization through an acquisition and a merger without losing personnel
- Developed "can-do approach" to problem solving and initiated ethics training
- Established management recruiting methods
- Created and presented training for marginal sales representatives
- Formulated computer programs to monitor performance in key areas of the business
- Elected to the Board of Directors of Home Mutual Life

EQUITABLE LIFE OF MO, St. Louis, MO   (1962-1985)
(Advanced from Sales Associate to Senior Vice President)

Senior Vice President – District Agencies   (1981-1985)
Directed field force of 650 people in sales, training, management, and recruiting. Effectively directed Home Office training, sales promotion, auditing, and human resources units.

SELECTED ACCOMPLISHMENTS:

- Increased field productivity by 10% annually
- Channeled sales efforts through innovative products
- Developed trusting employee relations atmosphere
- Proficiently taught management training program to home office middle management personnel

CARL J. EMILSON
Page Two

EQUITABLE LIFE OF MO, St. Louis, MO   (continued)

Regional Vice President   (1977-1981)

SELECTED ACCOMPLISHMENTS:

- Coordinated sales efforts of one of the two company regions
- Succeeded in moving the Midwest region to leadership in the company
- Achieved leading position in Western region after challenging transfer

District Sales Manager   (1975-1977)

SELECTED ACCOMPLISHMENTS:

- Led district to top 10% of the company's districts
- Positioned office for new sources of continuing revenue

Director of Training   (1974-1975)

Training Supervisor   (1972-1974)

Sales Manager   (1968-1972)

Sales Representative   (1962-1968)

EDUCATION/CERTIFICATION

Southern Indiana College, Indianapolis, IN (1957-1960)
Main Event Management Institute: Certified Instructor

MILITARY

US Army and Indiana National Guard   (1960-1966)

AFFILIATIONS/MEMBERSHIPS

Life Insurance Marketing Research Association
Life Insurers Conference
Arthritic Foundation – Board Member
National Association of Life Underwriters

TECHNICAL SKILLS

Microsoft Word, Lotus 123, WordPerfect